THE CLASSROOM TEACHER'S GUIDE
TO MUSIC EDUCATION

About the Author

Vernon Burnsed is Professor of Music and Coordinator of Music Education at Virginia Polytechnic Institute and State University where he teaches undergraduate and graduate music education and research courses, and works closely with public school personnel in field experiences for music education students Dr. Burnsed is an active researcher. He has written articles for the major research journals in music education and given research presentations at national and international conferences in the United States, Europe, and Africa.

THE CLASSROOM TEACHER'S GUIDE TO MUSIC EDUCATION

Second Edition

By

C. VERNON BURNSED, PH.D.

Associate Professor of Music
Virginia Polytechnic Institute and State University
Blacksburg, Virginia

CHARLES C THOMAS • PUBLISHER, LTD.
Springfield • Illinois • U.S.A.

Published and Distributed Throughout the World by
CHARLES C THOMAS · PUBLISHER, LTD.
2600 South First Street
Springfield, Illinois 62704

© *1999 by* CHARLES C THOMAS · PUBLISHER, LTD.
ISBN 0-398-06909-3 (spiral, paper)

Library of Congress Catalog Card Number: 98-14203

With THOMAS BOOKS *careful attention is given to all details of manufacturing
and design. It is the Publisher's desire to present books that are satisfactory as to their
physical qualities and artistic possibilities and appropriate for their particular use.*
THOMAS BOOKS *will be true to those laws of quality that assure a good name
and good will.*

Printed in the United States of America
CR-R-3

Library of Congress Cataloging in Publication Data

Burnsed, Charles Vernon.
 The classroom teacher's guide to music education / by C.
Vernon Burnsed. -- 2nd ed.
  p.   cm.
 Includes bibliographical references (p.   ) and index.
 ISBN (invalid) 0-398-06909-3 (spiral/paper)
 1. School music--Instruction and study. I. Title.
MT1.B87 1998
372.87'044--dc21   98-14203
                                                              CIP
                                                              MN

To
Tyra S. Burnsed and Coleen Grumley

PREFACE TO THE SECOND EDITION

The second edition includes contemporary thought on the philosophical rationales for music education, results of recent research in music education, and an expanded Chapter 5 on Music to Enhance the Learning Environment. Chapter 5 includes new greeting songs, a section on using music to teach topics and concepts throughout the elementary curriculum, and more suggestions for music and language arts. New songs are also included in the folk song appendix.

INTRODUCTION

This book is about music education in the elementary school. Its major purpose is to develop an understanding of why music education is important, how music education works, and how music can be a powerful force for the classroom teacher. It has realistic expectations for the classroom teacher. Music theory and performance skill are kept to a minimum; they are not a prerequisite for understanding the content of the book. The elements of music are presented through classroom activities very similar to those that occur in typical elementary music classes.

The text does not attempt to persuade the classroom teacher to teach music. Instead, it focuses on developing a broad perspective of elementary music education, and it illustrates how classroom teachers may use music as a powerful learning tool. A major emphasis of the text is that classroom teachers can utilize music to enhance the overall learning environment of their classrooms. Suggestions, class descriptions, and lesson plans are given for using music for routine activities, whole language, integrating music into language arts and social studies, and using music to develop the cultural literacy of students.

After completing the material in this text, students should understand the philosophical rationale for including music education in the public school. They should also be able to describe elementary music concepts and objectives for music education, discuss the Orff and Kodaly approaches to music education, and use music throughout the day to enhance the learning environment. With the proper in-class activities, the students should also develop competence in and positive attitudes about singing, and they should be able to provide children with quality musical experiences.

Singing and the Classroom Teacher

One of the most important outcomes of a music class for future classroom teachers should be the development of positive attitudes about singing. If classroom teachers can feel comfortable singing with their students, they can accomplish much. Singing with children throughout the day can be a powerful classroom tool, and if it is done with the proper attention to voice quality and pitch, it can be a very positive influence on the musical development of young children.

Unfortunately, singing skill cannot be developed by reading a book. However, proper singing technique and positive attitudes about singing can be accomplished without an overemphasis on theory. It has been the author's experience that positive attitudes and feelings of competence about singing can be developed through singing, moving, and playing music in much the same manner as music is taught in the elementary schools. The course instructor is encouraged to use the Curwen hand signs, "movable do," pentatonic patterns, and rote songs to develop the singing skill of the class participants.

Text Organization

The material in this text is presented as follows: music education philosophy and practice; understanding the elements of music; child development and learning theory in music; contemporary approaches to elementary music education; and music to enhance the learning environment. When possible the material is validated by the results of contemporary research in music education.

Recommendations are made for classroom activities and songs and materials are provided; however, the instructor may wish to supplement the text with other songs, Kodaly, Orff, and listening activities. In many instances specific resources are suggested.

A sequential arrangement of folk songs is included with the text. Each song is to reinforce the tonal and rhythm patterns presented throughout the text. If possible, the instructor should teach many of the songs by rote before utilizing their notated forms. After students have developed an aural awareness of the patterns in the songs, then a visual association may be made. As they progress through the text, students should label all the pitches of the songs and practice singing them with "movable do."

ACKNOWLEDGMENTS

I am most grateful to my students and colleagues for their many contributions to this text. In particular, I wish to thank Dr. Pamela Hopton Jones for suggestions and contributions to Chapter 5 of this edition. I also express my sincere thanks to the music and classroom teachers of Montgomery County, Virginia and to Myles and Linda Burnsed.

CONTENTS

Page

Preface to the Second Edition   vii
Introduction   ix

Chapter

1. MUSIC EDUCATION PHILOSOPHY AND PRACTICE   3

   Why Music Education   3
       Aesthetic Thinking   4
       Music as Procedureal Knowledge   4
       Utilitarian Rationales for Music Education   5
       The Role of the Music Education Specialist   7
       The Outcomes of Music Education   7
       The Value of Art Music   7
       Music to Enhance the Quality of Life   8

   Music Education in the Elementary School   8
       A Typical Lesson   9

   Chapter Summary   14
       Class Activities   15

   Suggested Resources   15

2. UNDERSTANDING THE ELEMENTS OF MUSIC   17

   Rhythm   17
       Pulse, Accent, Meter, and Patterns   18
           Class Activities   21
       Dotted Patterns and Syncopation   22
           Class Activities   24
       Compound Meter   24

Reading Rhythm   25
Multimeter and Polymeter   25
   Class Activities   26
Rhythm Summary   27
   Goals and Objectives for Rhythm in the
      Elementary School   28

Melody   28
   Pitch and Contour   29
   Melodic Patterns and Tonality   31
   Reading Melody   33
   Melody Summary   34
      Goals and Objectives for Melody in the Elementary
         School   35
      Class Activities   35

Harmony   37
   Harmonic Perception and Performance   38
   Chords, Intervals, and Triads   40
   Harmony Summary   42
      Goals and Objectives for Harmony in the
         Elementary School   42
      Class Activities   42

Form in Music   43
   The Primary Elements of Form   43
   Same and Different Phrases   44
   Binary and Ternary Form   45
   Other Forms   47
   Form Summary   48
      Goals and Objectives for Form in the Elementary
         School   48
      Class Activities   49

Timbre   49
   Exploring Sound   50
   The Instruments of the Orchestra   51
   Electronic and Vocal Timbres   52
   Timbre Summary   53

Goals and Objectives for Timbre in the Elementary
School 53
Class Activities 53

Expression in Music 54
Musical Performance Directions 54
Expression Summary 55
Goals and Objectives for Expression in the
Elementary School 55
Class Activities 56
Chapter Summary 57

Suggested Resources 57

3. CHILD DEVELOPMENT AND PRINCIPLES FOR 59
LEARNING MUSIC

Perceptual Development and Concept Formation 60

The Development of Performance Skill 62

Fostering the Development of Movement Skill 64
Rhythmic Sensitivity 67

The Development of Singing Skill 69
Principles for Teaching Singing 71
Selecting Songs for Young Children 72
Teaching a New Song 73

Musical Experiences for Early Childhood 75

Guidelines for Singing and Moving in the 76
Elementary School

The Development of Music Preference 77

Principles for Learning Music 78

Chapter Summary 79
Class Activities 80

Suggested Resources   82

4. CONTEMPORARY APPROACHES TO ELEMENTARY   83
   MUSIC EDUCATION

   The Kodaly Method   83
      Characteristics of the Kodaly Method   84
      The Pedagogical Process   87

   The Orff Process   90
      Characteristics of the Orff Process   90
      The Pedagogical Process   91
         Imitation   91
         Guided Exploration   92
         Improvisation   92
      Goals of the Orff Process   94

   Music Textbook Series   97
      Goals, Objectives, and Organization   97
      Songs and Recordings   98
      Listening Lessons and Guides   99
      Music Textbook Series in the Classroom   102

   Chapter Summary   104
      Suggested Activities   105

   Suggested Resources   106

5. MUSIC TO ENHANCE THE LEARNING ENVIRONMENT   109

   The Power of Music   109
   Music Throughout the Day   111

   Singing Games and Movement Activities   117
      Managing Movement Activites   117
      Movement and Basic Skills   119

   Creating Special Songs and Chants   120

Integrating Music into the Curriculum   123
    Class Activity   125
    Music and Language Arts   130
        Whole Language   133
        Music and Poetry   137
        Music and Children's Literature   137
        Music Listening and Language   138
    Music and Social Studies   139
    Other Integrative Categories   143
    Planning and Integration   144

Cultural Literacy in the Classroom   144
    Classics for the Classroom   147
    Jazz Classics   154

Chapter Summary   155
    Class Activities   155

Suggested Recordings   156

References   157

Appendices

    Common Key Signatures   158
    Folk Song Appendix   159
    Glossary of Selected Musical Terms   175

Subject Index   177
Song Index   182

THE CLASSROOM TEACHER'S GUIDE
TO MUSIC EDUCATION

Chapter 1

MUSIC EDUCATION PHILOSOPHY AND PRACTICE

WHY MUSIC EDUCATION?

One of the most important goals of this book is for the reader to understand why music education is an important part of schooling. Although most people will readily agree that they like and value music, many do not understand the role of music in education. Subsequently, in curricular and budget considerations, music is often regulated to a secondary or frill position in our schools.

There are a number of reasons for this phenomenon. One is that many music programs in public schools are actually selective performance group programs. This is especially true in the secondary school where unless students are in band, chorus, or orchestra, they may not receive any music instruction. This selectivity adds to the perception by many that music is only for the talented few.

Another reason many people do not understand the value of music education is that they are unable to see how knowledge and skill in music are essential for successful personal development. After all, you do not need to be able to sing to get most jobs, and music really does not help you balance your check book. To these people music education appears to be just entertainment.

Why then, is music education an important part of schooling? For many years it has been argued that music is included in the schools because music education is aesthetic education and its primary goal is to develop each individual's aesthetic sensitivity to music. Aesthetic education is the study of the nature of art and artistic properties. It involves perception, expression, imagination, and emotional reaction; it leads to the development of aesthetic sensitivity.

Aesthetic sensitivity is the ability to perceive and react to objects and events in life for their artistic properties and qualities. These objects and events may or may not be works of art. One may contemplate buildings for

3

their design, scenery for color and line, and the sounds of nature for patterns and timbres. This aesthetic manner of thinking and perceiving enhances living. It satisfies a basic human need, the aspiration for something more than just survival.

Aesthetic Thinking

An important part of aesthetic education and aesthetic sensitivity is what some authors have called an aesthetic mode of thinking. This mode of perception and expression involves imagination, feeling, and the consideration of events and objects from a non-logical point of view. When one thinks in an aesthetic manner, the overall feeling of the thought or communication is more important than its rationale or logic. Consider the following expressions. The first is by Robert Burns; the second two are by Paul Simon.

you stole the rose and left the thorn

hello darkness my old friend

like a bridge over troubled water I will lay me down

It is easy to see how this type of thinking is creative and imaginative, and how a society needs aesthetic thinking and discovery just as a society needs scientific thinking and discovery. Aesthetic education enhances individual existence and a society's cultural development. One of the purposes of schooling is to enhance the lives of individuals, to help them reach their fullest potential. Thus it is readily observable how aesthetic education is an important part of public school education. People make aesthetic decisions every day of their lives. The quality of life not only depends on the material but the emotional.

A society's art records the emotional and feelingful aspects of living in that society. No other medium of expression expresses the feelings and emotion of the cultures of civilization. One can read about a culture but when one views its art and listens to its music one may actually experience the emotional life of that culture.

Music as Procedural Knowledge

Another philosophical basis for the value of music education is that musicing (performing music) is an important form of procedural knowledge.

When one performs music one is thinking and reflecting in action; one knows how to do something rather than knows about something. This knowledge in action is critical to cognitive, emotional, and psychomotor development. David Elliott (1995) believes that musicing is essential to enable self-growth, self-knowledge, and optimal experience. According to Elliott, it is only through musical performance and the development of musicianship that one can achieve the optimal musical experiences that can enhance self-knowledge, esteem, and the quality of living.

Elliott and others have used the term "flow" to characterize optimal experience. Flow occurs when one's attention becomes so focused on an activity that one becomes lost in the moment or unconscious of a separate self from the action. One experiences personal growth as a result of flow and life becomes more meaningful. Musical performance and listening to music can become a means of achieving flow and the resulting self-growth and awareness. Anyone who has participated in musically expressive performances more than likely has experienced flow. Some argue that flow and the aesthetic experience are the same. Others argue that they are different; however, what is important is that music can be an important source for a heightened awareness that enhances the quality of life.

It should be acknowledged that one need not be an expert performer to achieve flow as a result of musicing. Elliott points out that flow can be achieved when a challenge is presented and is capable of being reached. A match occurs between the performer's ability and the challenge that is presented. Therefore, an elementary general music class might be challenged to perform a simple round with instrumental accompaniment whereas a high school choir may be challenged to perform a Bach *cantata*. Each should have the capability of achieving the challenge and experience growth, increased ability, self-awareness, and self-esteem from the resulting flow or optimal experience.

Utilitarian Rationales for Music Education

There are also many utilitarian or nonmusical reasons for including music education in the public schools. Strong music and arts programs enhance the learning environment, make school more attractive, and are a source of pride and identity for the school community. Everyone is pleased to see and hear outstanding performances by the band, orchestra, or chorus at community and athletic events and competitions. These performances encourage positive thoughts about the quality of school systems and are great public relations tools for administrators. Even in the elementary school, music performance may be a primary goal of music education. Musical presentations for PTA meetings and special holiday programs are common.

Another reason for including music education in the public schools is that music in itself is an academic discipline. It has structure, tradition, and history. If one were to analyze the learning activities that occur in music education one would find a very high level of cognitive, affective, and psychomotor learning. Some research even indicates that music education enhances reading skill, creativity, and spatial intelligence. Just listening to Mozart has been shown to raise IQ scores and students who study music in early childhood have demonstrated increased spatial reasoning when compared to those who do not study music. Other research indicates that when the arts are integrated into the core curriculum, overall academic achievement is positively affected and school vandalism and truancy are lessened. Music has also been found to be a powerful reward for learning and achievement, and many people speak about the positive effects of working in music groups towards a common goal.

During the late seventies, there was much call for a "back to the basics" in school curriculums. This movement threatened the place of music in the school for those who considered music nonacademic or as a frill. However, if one defines basic as something that is a fundamental aspect of living, then music is surely basic. For example, research has shown that there is a biological basis for music in humans and animals. Our brains are constructed to do music. Everyone actually sings before they begin to speak (indeed infant singing may help us learn to speak) and neonates and infants perceive pitch, rhythm, and contour in music. Harvard psychologist Howard Gardner believes that music intelligence is one of seven basic intelligences which are present in all humans.

No known civilization has ever existed without music and art. Contemporary society is inundated with music virtually twenty four hours a day. When one considers the prevalence of music in society one may wonder if society could exist without music. Not surprisingly, all the various commissions and studies of reform in education during the 80s (Adler, 1982; Gardner, 1983; Boyer, 1983; College Entrance Board, 1983; Goodlad, 1984; Bennett, 1987) have recommended the study of the arts.

All of the above reasons are valid and important reasons for including music education in the school. Indeed, when one realizes all of the very positive benefits of music education, one wonders why there is ever a question of its value. Unfortunately, music is usually taught only once or twice a week in the elementary school for a total of about 40 minutes of music instruction a week. This occurs, if the school has a music specialist. If not, music may comprise very little of the school week. Research indicates that very few classroom teachers spend more than five minutes a day with music. These observations lead one to wonder whether school systems really recognize the value of music education in the schooling of all children.

The Role of the Music Education Specialist

In the preceding discussion one of the primary purposes of music education in the schools was defined as being the development of each individual's aesthetic sensitivity to music. To understand how this purpose can be achieved refer to the definition of aesthetic sensitivity.

Aesthetic sensitivity is the ability to perceive and react to objects and events in life for their artistic properties and qualities.

The key part, "the ability to perceive" actually indicates what the music education specialist is trying to achieve. The music educator is attempting to increase student ability to perceive the artistic properties and qualities of music. These properties and qualities are usually referred to as the elements or concepts of music. They include melody, rhythm, harmony, form, volume, tempo, timbre, and the underlying percepts that make up these concepts. The study of these concepts and percepts is achieved primarily through musical performance and aural perception. Students are led to discover how the elements of music are combined and manipulated by the composer to create musical expression as they learn to sing, play instruments, and move to music.

The Outcomes of Music Education

The end result of music instruction as defined above should be fundamental performance skill and the ability to listen to various styles of music and describe how the composer manipulated the elements of music to create expression and emotional effect. This performance and perceptual skill affects one's music preference and the emotional reaction that results from listening to music. One becomes more sensitive to the aesthetic quality of music. Increased perceptual skill may increase one's liking for some musics and decrease liking for other musics. This is even true for art music. However, an important outcome of music education should be the ability to listen to and understand (some say appreciate) art music.

The Value of Art Music

Art music is music that is recognized as great music by experts, scholars, and musicians. This music may have existed for centuries like Bach or

Beethoven or it may be contemporary electronic music or jazz, and even in some cases rock and folk music. The one characteristic that ties these different styles together as art music is expressive content. This expressive content is created through structural properties which involve simple versus complex, expected versus surprising, and familiar versus unfamiliar combinations of tonal and rhythm patterns. Art music has expressive content which is created by the way the music is constructed.

In contrast, popular music contains one or two dominant elements, usually rhythm and melody, and it contains very few surprises. The primary structural characteristic is usually repetition. Because of this simplicity, popular music does not stay popular very long and it does not stimulate aesthetic reaction beyond the first two or three hearings. On the other hand, art music is complex, has great expressive content, and can stimulate a wide range of aesthetic reactions over repeated listening. Because of its complexity, art music has more potential for aesthetic response and optimal experience.

This complexity also is the reason many people do not listen to art music. They do not have the perceptual skill to understand this music. Thus, a goal of music education is to develop the perceptual skill needed to respond to the aesthetic content of all musics and in particular art music. Heightened perceptual skills in music will allow students to make intelligent aesthetic judgments about all musics. Music performance or musicing (Elliott, 1995) plays an important role in developing this perceptual skill.

Music to Enhance the Quality of Life

Another outcome of music education should be continued interest in music for both performing and listening enjoyment. Musically educated people not only are aesthetically sensitive to music but they continually seek out a variety of musical experiences and in general use music to enhance the quality of their lives. They may enjoy performing music in community bands, orchestras, and choruses or perhaps they perform piano and guitar individually or with small groups. Perhaps they do not perform, but attend concert series, public performances, and they have a substantial collection of recordings of a variety of musics for both individual and social listening activities at home.

MUSIC EDUCATION IN THE ELEMENTARY SCHOOL

To understand how the music education specialist develops aesthetic sensitivity and musical understanding consider a typical elementary music lesson. As mentioned previously, the music specialist may meet with students twice a week for approximately twenty minutes each meeting. This is not much time to teach anything, much less something as complex as music. Nevertheless, some music educators achieve much within this limited amount of time. In the elementary school, performance (as in a concert) should not be the main outcome of the music class, but the music class must include performance activity. Performance is a primary means for learning and experiencing music. It is hard to imagine young children sitting still to listen to lectures about music. The music class is usually taught through singing, moving, playing instruments, and listening.

A Typical Lesson

Consider a typical music class for second grade children. Assume that the music specialist has a music room and a moderate amount of materials. First, the children come into the class and sit on the floor. An ideal music room will have a carpet for the children to sit on. The children may sit in a circle or in designated places in rows.

The music teacher will probably begin singing to the children as they enter the class. This first song may be as simple as "Come and sing your name for me" or "Hello who are you" or a familiar tune. The important criterion is that the first song/activity be something that everyone can participate in successfully. Immediately after the first song, the music teacher asks the children to echo sing the melodic patterns *sol mi sol la sol mi*. The teacher and the children will accompany the patterns with hand signs.

The music teacher then asks the class to sing the familiar song *Acka Backa*. The teacher and the children "pat clap" the pulse as they sing *Acka Backa*, then they clap the pattern of the melody. Next the teacher sings *Acka Backa* with hand signs and asks the children to identify *sol la sol mi* in this familiar tune. The class is then shown *sol la sol mi* on a two line staff on the chalk board. The teacher and children practice singing *sol la sol mi* from the staff.

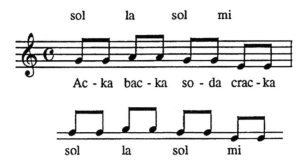

Next the teacher leads the children in the familiar song *Kookaburra*. The children "pat clap" the pulse as they sing the song in unison and then as a round. The teacher asks if anyone can find *sol la sol mi* in *Kookaburra*. The teacher helps the class discover the *sol la sol mi* pattern of the first phrase of *Kookaburra*. Next the teacher and class count the phrases in *Kookaburra* and the teacher asks the class if the first two phrases are "like or different" from the third and fourth phrases. The class responds "different" and the teacher labels the first two phrases as A and the last two as B. The teacher concludes that *Kookaburra* is in simple binary form.

Kookaburra

The teacher next asks the class to echo clap some rhythm patterns. They clap simple rhythm patterns similar to those in *Acka Backa*. The teacher then draws the primary rhythm pattern of *Acka Backa* on the board. The children practice clapping and chanting the pattern.

The teacher introduces the new song *Rocky Mountain* by singing it through. She asks the students to sing along and clap the pulse and then the rhythm pattern of the melody. They discover that the melody moves in a rhythm pattern like *Acka Backa* (in fact the first phrase of each has the same rhythm pattern) and that *Rocky Mountain* is also in simple binary form (AB) like *Kookaburra*. This song will be used later as a folk dance and also to introduce singing in harmony

Rocky Mountain

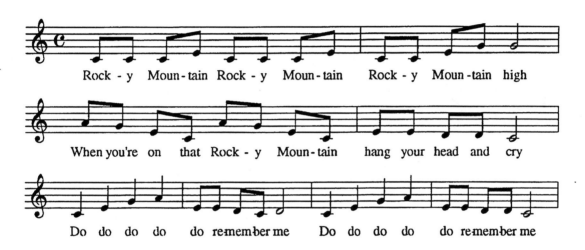

The next activity of the music class would very likely be a movement activity. This activity might be to recorded music, the teacher playing the piano, or movement to the children's own singing. The movement will focus on interpreting the music expressively, in a design sense (different movements for the verse and refrain), or interpreting the words of a game song, folk or square dance. The children all enjoy moving to the music; it is obvious that this is a very popular activity

The class might conclude with a listening activity. The teacher tells the class that they will hear an orchestra piece titled *In the Hall of the Mountain King* by Edvard Grieg. The teacher first asks the class to listen for repetition and for change. "What repeats and what changes?" After one hearing, the teacher asks the class if they have heard the piece before. Many may have. It is a very popular classical work. The class readily identifies that the rhythm and melody are constantly repeated throughout the work and that the tempo, dynamics, and instrumental timbre change. The class listens a second time as the teacher directs their attention to the following listening guide on the board.

In the Hall of the Mountain King

pp   *ff*

Accel.

If there is time, the class might conclude with a familiar song or the teacher may play another orchestra piece similar to the Grieg as the children line up to return to their regular classroom. To review this lesson, first look at the lesson plan.

Lesson Plan

Concepts/Percepts

Melody—patterns *sol mi, sol la sol mi*
Rhythm—pulse, *ti ti*
Form—phrases, simple binary
Timbre—strings, bassoon, full orchestra texture
Expression—tempo, dynamics, timbre

Objectives

to sing melodic patterns accurately with hand signs and on staff (*sol la sol mi*)
to identify *sol la sol mi* in familiar songs and on staff
to echo clap and identify *ti ti* patterns
to identify phrases in *Acka Backa* and *Kookaburra*
to identify *Kookaburra* as binary (AB) (also *Rocky Mountain* & *Yankee Doodle*)
to introduce *Rocky Mountain* and identify *ti ti* pattern
to move to the pulse of "Walking Notes"
to identify changes in tempo, dynamics, and instrumentation in *Hall of the Mountain King*

Materials

Recordings of *In the Hall of the Mountain King, Variations on Simple Gifts,* and Hap Palmer's "Walking Notes" from *The Feel of Music*

Chalk board—two line staff, rhythm patterns, Accel., Cresc.

Procedures

Greeting—*Come and sing* as the children enter, match pitch
Hand sing *sol mi, sol la sol mi*

Familiar Songs—*Acka Backa*—Sing expressively with attention to phrasing and dynamics, pat clap the pulse, clap rhythm pattern, count phrases, identify *sol la sol mi* in tune and on two line staff. *Kookaburra*—Sing expressively in unison, then as a round, pat clap pulse, count phrases, compare phrases and discover form (AB), identify *sol la sol mi* in tune and on two line staff.

Echo Clap—*ti ti* patterns from *Acka Backa*, identify pattern on board.

New Song—*Rocky Mountain*—Sing through, discuss, all sing together, by phrases if needed, sing and pat the pulse, clap the pattern. Is the rhythm pattern like *Acka Backa*?

Movement Activity—Hap Palmer "Walking Notes" Find your own space, explore so that you can't touch, freeze when the music stops, play, when stopped, choose good movers as leaders for wandering snake patterns.

Listening—*In the Hall of the Mountain King* by Grieg from *Peer Gynt Suite*. Today we are going to listen to a very famous piece by Grieg called *In the Hall of the Mountain King*, some of you may have heard it before, as we listen, listen for repetition and things that change. *Play one time.* Who has heard it before? What stays the same (is repeated)? Point to rhythm pattern. What changes? Tempo, dynamics, point to cresc., and accelerando designations on board. *Play again.* What else changes? Help the children discover different timbres (strings, bassoon, etc.).

Familiar Song—*Yankee Doodle*—Sing through, clap and identify even pattern of ti ti, count phrases, identify as AB form.

Closure—Let's review, sing *sol la sol mi* on staff, clap *ti ti* patterns. What kind of form is *Kookaburra*? Can you identify other songs that are AB? (*Rocky Mountain*) As we line up to go out, let's listen to another piece of music that has lots of repetition. (*Copland, Variations on Simple Gifts*).

What did the teacher actually teach in this lesson? How was aesthetic sensitivity and musical understanding developed? First consider what elements were taught or presented. These are listed at the beginning of the lesson plan under concepts. All of the elements of music except harmony were presented in this lesson (Actually harmony was presented in the singing of the round *Kookaburra*). The melodic and singing teaching focused on the perception of melodic patterns (*sol mi sol la sol mi*). Echo clapping, keeping the pulse, and identifying rhythm patterns were utilized to develop the children's perceptual and performance skills in rhythm.

Perceiving form (the design) in music was presented in the singing and listening segments. Identifying phrases and like and different sections are important steps in perceiving the design of music. The perception of timbre was presented in the listening segment and the repetition of the melody with changing tempos, timbres, and dynamics was identified as an expressive device in the Grieg selection. Expression was also created by expressive movement and singing in the other segments of the lesson. Learning to sing and move expressively to music and identifying and discriminating between the elements and percepts of melody, rhythm, form, timbre and expression will lead to the development of aesthetic sensitivity and musical understanding.

CHAPTER SUMMARY

There are many important reasons for including music in the public schools. A primary purpose of music education is to develop aesthetic sensitivity to music. Aesthetic sensitivity is defined as the ability to perceive and react to the objects and events in life for their artistic properties and qualities. Aesthetic sensitivity to music is the ability to perceive the concepts and underlying percepts of music and the ensuing emotional reaction to how these concepts and percepts are manipulated by the composer to create expression. The study of musical performance and the development of fundamental musicianship is also an important part of music education. This "musicing" leads to optimal experience and flow with music which develops self-knowledge, esteem, and enhances the quality of life. Music education is also an important part of cultural sophistication and transformation. Research has also shown that music education develops overall cognitive abilities that contribute to reading and spatial awareness.

The role of the music specialist in the public schools is to teach perception of the elements of music and the manipulation of these elements by composers. This perception which is primarily aural is taught through singing, moving, playing instruments, and listening to music. The quality of the music and these experiences is very important in the development of aesthetic sensitivity and musical understanding. Art music has more potential for aesthetic reaction than popular music. Therefore, an important part of music education is exposure to art music. All music performance and teaching must be done with sensitivity and attention to the emotional expression in music.

Class Activities

1. Discuss the purpose of music in your own education. Do you believe that its primary purpose was aesthetic education? If not, what were the primary outcomes of your own music education?

2. Give all the possible rationales for including music in the school curriculum. Is music basic? What are some positive nonmusical outcomes of music education?

3. Observe an elementary music class. What concepts and percepts were taught? Did the class focus on the expression in music?

4. Review published music lesson plans in music textbook series. How do they develop aesthetic sensitivity? Do they teach performance?

5. Interview a music education specialist and a classroom teacher about the purposes of music education in the schools. How often does the classroom teacher teach music?

6. Listen to a current "top forty" song and compare it to a movement of a Mozart or Beethoven symphony. Contrast the repetition, variety, and complexity of the two types of music.

SUGGESTED RESOURCES

Adler, M. J. (1982). *The paideia proposal.* New York: Macmillan.
Bennett, W.J. (1987). *James Madison high school: A curriculum for American students.* Washington, D.C.: U. S. Department of Education.
Boyer, E. L. (1983). *High school: A report on secondary education in America.* New York: Harper and Row.

Broudy, H. S. (1978). How basic is aesthetic education? Is 'RT the fourth R? *Bulletin of the Council for Research in Music Education, 57,* 1 -11.

College Entrance Board (1983). *Academic preparation for college: What students need to know and be able to do.* New York: Educational Quality Project.

Elliott, D. J. (1995). *Music matters: A new philosophy of music education.* NY: Oxford University Press.

Gardner, D. P. (1983). *A nation at risk: The imperative for educational reform.* Washington, D.C.: National Commission on Excellence in Education, United States Department of Education.

Gardner, H. (1983). *Frames of mind: The Theory of Multiple Intelligences.* NY: Basic Books.

Goodlad, J. I. (1984). *A place called school.* New York: McGraw-Hill.

Weinberger, N. M. (1994). The musical infant. *MuSICA Research Notes,* I(1), Spring 1994, 1.

Weinberger, N. M. (1994). Music and cognitive achievement in children. *MuSICA Research Notes,* I(2), Fall 1994, 1.

Weinberger, N. M. (1995). The nonmusical outcomes of music education. *MuSICA Research Notes,* II(2), Fall 1995, 1.

Weinberger, N. M. (1996). Sing sing sing. *MuSICA Research Notes,* III(2), Fall 1996, 1.

Wolff, K. L. (1978). The nonmusical outcomes of music education: a review of the literature. *Bulletin of the Council for Research in Music Education, 55,* 1-27.

Chapter 2

UNDERSTANDING THE ELEMENTS OF MUSIC

To be aesthetically sensitive to music, students must be able to perceive the artistic properties of music. These properties, often called the elements of music, are the concepts of melody, harmony, rhythm, form, timbre, and expression. When we hear music we hear the underlying percepts of these concepts and how the composer has manipulated them to create expression. A fundamental part of aesthetic perception is the ability to perceive these components and their interaction in music.

There are many underlying percepts of each of the above mentioned concepts. The more sophisticated one's perceptual skills become, the more one is able to perceive. For convenience, this chapter will discuss the above elements of music at an elementary level. The reader will become familiar with the elements of music and their percepts as they are taught in typical elementary music programs. This is by no means, however, a complete analysis of the elements of music. The study of the interaction of the elements of music becomes very sophisticated at the secondary level and above.

RHYTHM

Rhythm is probably the most dominant element in popular music today and also the easiest element of music for most people to perceive. Many people refer to the beat of favorite recordings and everyone claps along with the bands at social and athletic events. In fact, the "right" rhythm is probably the single most important element in popular music today. The rhythm of music is also very important in determining moods, selling products, worker productivity, and a number of other everyday events in our lives. Psychologists have long recognized the power of rhythm to affect human activity. What is rhythm?

Rhythm in music is the organization of sounds and silences into patterns. There are many examples of rhythm throughout the natural environment that are not part of music. One may hear the rhythm of rain, automobile tires on the highway, and the wind in trees. There are even philosophical theories about the rhythm of the ebb and flow of living. Life is permeated with rhythm within and without music. Perhaps this is why rhythm in music affects humans so easily.

Pulse, Accent, Meter, and Patterns

When people move to music they are usually moving to the pulse of the rhythm of the music. This is the regularly occurring beat that is felt during marching, clapping, or dancing to music. These pulses are grouped by accents into twos or threes which form meter in music. The following example represents duple meter, pulses grouped in twos by alternating accents.

This could also be represented by chanting <u>ta</u> ta <u>ta</u> ta <u>ta</u> ta (underline indicates accent). Triple meter can be represented similarly.

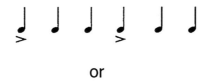

or

<u>ta</u> ta ta <u>ta</u> ta ta

Triple meter is often perceived as a waltz whereas duple is more related to walking or marching. Just about all the music of western civilization is in duple or triple meter or a combination of the two.

There are many activities for teaching the perception of pulse, accent, and meter to kindergarten and elementary age children. Most of these utilize movement in some way or another. Children are often asked to move to the beat or clap the beat. Unfortunately, research indicates that for very young children muscular coordination with the beat may be difficult. Chanting the beat on *ta* or a similar word may be a better teaching activity for developing a perception of the pulse with very young children. Moving to music is a very valuable activity at any age level; however, regular coordination with the pulse should not be a criterion for movement with young children. They will gradually develop skill in moving to the pulse as they grow and mature.

Sounds and silences are of different lengths in music and rhythm. This percept of rhythm is called duration and is often the focus of music reading activities. Notes and silences (rests) of different lengths are combined to form different patterns in music. The perception of patterns in music is very important to perceiving expression. Duration and patterns are taught in the elementary school through a variety of activities. Chanting different words of different lengths is one example.

By Grace C. Nash, Geraldine W. Jones, Barbara A. Potter and Patsy F. Smith from *Do It My Way, The Child's Way of Learning, A Handbook for Building Creative Teaching Experiences*. Copyright 1977 by Alfred Publishing Co., Inc. All Rights Reserved. Used by Permission of the Publisher.

The note values (duration) of the first line should be exactly twice as long as the note values of the second. Music educators guide children to explore different combinations of words to discover their duration relationship. The following duration chart shows common rhythmic relationships.

Duration Chart

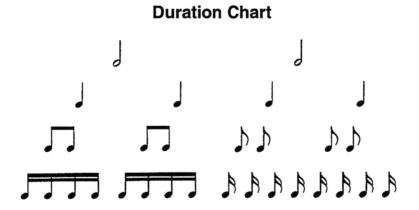

Notes of different duration values are combined in music to create different levels of rhythm patterns. Today, most music educators utilize a system of verbal association to teach different durations and patterns. A word or word syllable is utilized to represent a certain duration or combination of duration values that create a pattern. The following chart gives some commonly used words and word syllables and their accompanying patterns.

Word Syllables and Rhythm Patterns

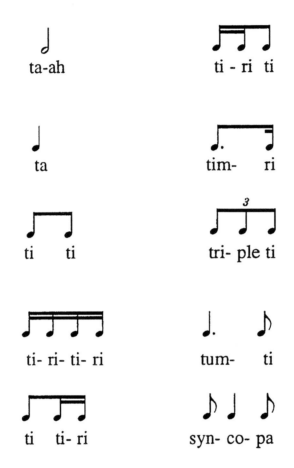

ta-ah	ti - ri ti
ta	tim- ri
ti ti	tri- ple ti
ti- ri- ti- ri	tum- ti
ti ti- ri	syn- co- pa

All of the above patterns are present in young children's music and are easily learned when presented in the proper sequence. Music educators first teach children familiar songs which include the patterns. After the students have a proper aural concept of a pattern, a symbol is assigned to it. Children might learn the pattern *ti ti* by singing and clapping *Yankee Doodle*. After they are familiar with the song, the music teacher points out that the rhythm of the words (melody) is *ti ti ti ti ti ti ti ti ti ti ti ti ta ta*. Then the students practice the rhythm syllables and identify them in other familiar tunes like *Are You Sleeping*. The teacher then gives a visual representation (stick notation) of the rhythm pattern.

Stick Notation

ti ti   ti ti   ti ti   ti ti   ti ti   ta   ti   ti ta

Other rhythm patterns are presented in a similar manner. The pattern *tir-itiri* (four even sounds to a pulse) occurs in the popular songs *Kookaburra* and *Are You Sleeping*. More will be presented about the proper sequence of teaching rhythm and other percepts in Chapter Four when the methods of Kodaly and Orff are discussed.

Class Activities

1. Practice moving and clapping the pulse to different song recordings in different meters.

2. Chant and then clap the following words and their rhythm to discover the duration values and rhythmic patterns.

Apples peaches apricots
Strawberries oranges nectarines

You should have discovered the following duration values and patterns.

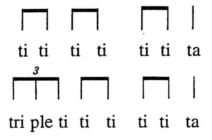

ti ti   ti ti   ti ti   ta

tri ple ti ti ti   ti ti   ta

3. Practice the *tripleti* versus the *ti ti*. Perceiving the difference between these two patterns is very important in developing perceptual skills in rhythm. For more experience with *tripleti* and *ti ti*, chant and clap the patterns of *Doctor Foster*.

Doctor Foster

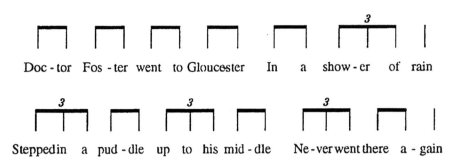

Doc - tor Fos - ter went to Gloucester   In   a   show - er   of rain

Stepped in a pud - dle up to his mid - dle   Ne - ver went there a - gain

4. What are some other chants with *tripleti*? An elementary music specialist might use the following words to teach rhythm patterns to young children. Can you think of other word rhythms?

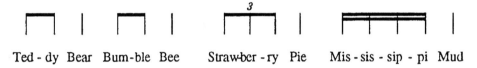

Ted - dy Bear Bum-ble Bee   Straw-ber - ry Pie   Mis - sis - sip - pi Mud

5. Practice chanting, clapping, and echo clapping different combinations of the patterns illustrated in the Word Syllables and Rhythm Patterns chart on page 20. For example *ti ti ta ti ti ta* and *tiritiri tiritiri ti ti ta*. Write different rhythm patterns on flash cards and practice clapping and chanting them with a partner.

6. Sing many familiar songs and discover their rhythm patterns. For example, *Are You Sleeping* includes *ti ti ti ti, ti ti ta*, and *tiritiri ti ti*. Where do these patterns occur? Can you write them in stick notation?

7. Perform and write the patterns to the following songs: *Kookaburra, This Old Man,* and *Chatter with the Angels.* (See Folk Song Appendix)

Dotted Patterns and Syncopation

As children develop skill in identifying, writing, and performing patterns which include *ti ti, tripleti,* and *tiritiri*, dotted and syncopation patterns may be introduced. Dotted patterns get their characteristic sound from uneven divisions of the pulse. In the familiar *Yankee Doodle* the uneven division of the pulse (dotted pattern) occurs at the beginning of the chorus. The national anthem uses the dotted pattern in the beginning.

Yan-kee Doo-dle keep it up   O - h say can you see

Favorite songs like *Hear Ye the Wind is Rising* and *Clapping Land* (Folk Song Appendix) develop perception of dotted patterns. Another common dotted pattern occurs in *America the Beautiful*.

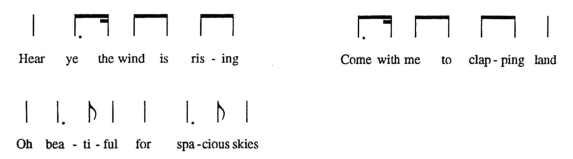

Hear   ye   the wind is   ris - ing   Come with me   to   clap - ping land

Oh   bea - ti - ful   for   spa -cious skies

The dotted pattern is easily learned by young people when presented in the manner described previously -- singing familiar songs which include the pattern, then identifying the pattern.

Syncopation is when the rhythm pattern does not coincide with the pulse. Instead of the accents occurring with the pulse, they occur either before or after the pulse. Sometimes this is called accenting the up-beats or off-beats. *Shoo fly* is a good example of syncopation. "Shoo fly don't" represents the pattern *syn co pa*.

Syncopation

syn   co   pa

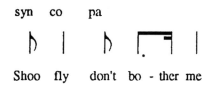

Shoo   fly   don't bo - ther me

The accented upbeat occurs on "fly" or "co". The folk song *Tom Dooley* also begins with *syn co pa*.

syn   co   pa

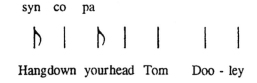

Hangdown yourhead Tom   Doo - ley

Popular music, rock, and jazz also have many syncopated rhythms.

Class Activities

1. Find elementary level songs with dotted patterns. Practice writing the patterns. Use the following procedure: Sing the song, clap the pattern, say the rhythm syllables (*timri*, etc.), then write the pattern.

2. Echo clap and write different dotted patterns and patterns with syncopation.

3. What songs can you find that use syncopation? Practice singing and clapping *Excerpt from Little David*.

Excerpt from Little David

Lit - tle Da - vid   play on   your   harp hal - le - lu hal - le -

lu   Lit - tle Da - vid   play on   your   harp hal - le - lu

Compound Meter

So far only patterns found in simple duple or triple meter have been discussed. These meters are characterized by duple divisions of the pulse. Another common meter is called compound meter; it is characterized by triple divisions of the pulse. The basic division of the pulse feels like *tripleti* rather than *ti ti*.

Compound Meter

Many learned compound meter as 6/8, 9/8, or 12/8 in school performance groups. *Row Row Your Boat* is a popular childhood song that is in compound meter. The rhythm pattern of the melody is the basic *tripleti* pattern, especially at "merrily merrily merrily merrily life is but a dream."

Row Row Your Boat

Mer-ri-ly mer-ri-ly   mer-ri-ly mer-ri-ly   Life is but   a   dream

This example gives the two most frequent patterns in compound meter: the *tripleti* and the *ta* followed by the single *ti* which also has a triple feel.

Reading Rhythm

As children become comfortable with identifying the different patterns associated with duple, triple, and compound meter music educators lead them to understand and interpret time signatures. The time signature is the mathematical fraction or "C" designation at the beginning of a written song that indicates how the time is measured. For example, 4/4 indicates that there are four quarter notes (tas) in a measure (the distance between two bar lines). To help young children identify the basic note value of measurement many elementary music educators use the following modified time signatures.

$$\frac{4}{\text{♩}} = \frac{4}{4} \text{ or } \mathbf{C} \qquad \frac{2}{\text{♩}} = \frac{2}{4} \qquad \frac{6}{\text{♪}} = \frac{6}{8} \qquad \frac{3}{\text{♩}} = \frac{3}{4} \qquad \frac{2}{\text{♩}} = \frac{2}{2} \text{ or } \mathbf{¢}$$

Often the bottom number or note is the basic pulse (gets one beat) for the music. This is not always true, however, and students should understand that different notes can be designated as the basic pulse with various time signatures. For example, 3/4 is often performed so that the basic pulse is a dotted half note, the equivalent of a whole measure in 3/4.

Multimeter and Polymeter

Sometimes the meter within a song changes as it is performed. This is an example of multimeter or changing meters. The Beatles used this technique in popular music. *Here Comes the Sun* and *All You Need is Love* are good examples of multimeter. Contemporary music composers often use the technique of polymeter in their compositions. This is when two or more meters occur simultaneously. *Petrushka* by Stravinsky is a good example of polymeter in contemporary music. Polymetric music is very difficult to perform and almost impossible to dance to. This difficulty is caused by the accents occurring on different pulses. Consider a combination of duple and triple meter.

Polymeter

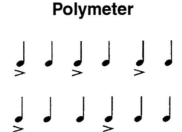

Observe how the accents are not uniform.

Class Activities

1. Practice singing and clapping *When Johnny Comes Marching Home* (See Folk Song Appendix). Can you write the compound meter patterns? Can you find the most common compound meter patterns in other compound meter tunes?

2. In addition to the many songs in compound meter there are rhymes and limericks that develop a feel for compound meter patterns. Practice the following limerick in 6/8 time.

There Was an Old Man With a Beard

by Edward Lear
arranged by Arlene Herndon

Ostinato

Underlined words

Snap on ( ) words

3. Divide the class, have one half clap in duple while the other half claps in triple. The pulse must be the same. Experience the polymeter feeling.

Rhythm Summary

As mentioned earlier, rhythm is probably the most dominant element in popular music and the most effective in terms of human response to music. Rhythm is the organization of sounds and silences grouped into patterns. Rhythm not only occurs in music but actually permeates human existence. People hear, feel, and see rhythm in various forms throughout their daily lives. Perhaps this is why rhythm in music has been shown to be so affective of the human condition.

Young children easily respond to rhythm in music. Although their movements may not be accurate reflections of the pulse and accompanying patterns, it is readily observable that they do respond to rhythm. Inaccuracy in rhythmic response in early childhood is usually a matter of psychomotor development and should not be a factor of great concern. However, it is very important that young children experience movement to rhythm in music. A variety of experiences with music in early childhood is crucial to the later development of perceptual skill in music.

The major percepts of rhythm are pulse, accent, meter, duration, and patterns. These percepts are presented through a variety of movement, listening, and performance activities. Unfortunately, many programs emphasize reading rhythm patterns before an aural sense of rhythm has been developed. This is similar to trying to read language without the proper aural sense of the symbols. Language is listened to in many forms long before the visual symbols of language are interpreted. Music must be presented similarly. Developing an aural sense of pulse, accent, meter, duration, and patterns is necessary for perceptual development in music.

Goals and Objectives for Rhythm in the Elementary School

The students will move expressively to the rhythm of the music

The students will chant, pat, and clap the pulse of the music

The students will echo chant and clap familiar rhythm patterns

The students will identify meter as duple or triple

The students will aurally identify and label rhythm patterns in familiar and unfamiliar music

The students will perform familiar rhythm patterns from notation

The students will continue to develop the ability to move and perform with rhythmic accuracy and sensitivity

MELODY

What is melody in music? People hum and sing favorite melodies but what is a melody? Melodies are perceived as horizontal entities or wholes. When one hears a melody one remembers the whole rather than the individual tones. Thus, a melody is a sequence of tones that is perceived as a whole. This sequence is generally thought of as horizontal, going across the page. The important aspect is that this sequence of tones is arranged so that it is perceived as a whole or unit.

Melodies are cultural phenomena in that what a person from a Western society perceives as melody may not be perceived as such by a person from another culture. A person from the Far East may have a different perception of melody than a Westerner. Western melodies generally are composed of intervals (the distance between two tones) that are close together whereas a melody from another culture might have wide intervals or intervals smaller than a half step, the smallest pitch interval in Western music. There are a number of other psychological principles that determine melody in Western music; however, this discussion will just refer to the definition of melody as a sequence of tones perceived as a whole.

Pitch and Contour

Melodies are made up of pitches. Therefore, the perception of melody begins with the perception of pitch. Pitch is the phenomenon that tones are perceived as higher or lower than one another. This phenomenon is caused by the differences in frequency of vibration of different sound waves which are created when different pitches are performed by striking, bowing, or blowing air through an instrument.

Young children are led to explore and experiment with pitch in a variety of ways. This sound exploration can lead to the development of concepts about the principles of sound production. Children may discover that big things sound low and little things sound high. Percepts of high and low are some of the first percepts of music to be presented to young children. Numerous activities are presented to aid young children in their development of an aural sense of high and low. The following tune may be accompanied with body movement.

I can sing up high   I can sing down low

By Grace C. Nash, Geraldine W. Jones, Barbara A. Potter and Patsy F. Smith from *Do It My Way, The Child's Way of Learning, A Handbook for Building Creative Teaching Experiences.* Copyright 1977 by Alfred Publishing Co., Inc. All Rights Reserved. Used by Permission of the Publisher.

Along with the perception of high and low, music teachers also encourage children to demonstrate how the melody moves. Does this melody go up, down, or stay the same? How does the melody move, in steps, skips, or leaps? These are questions that concern the contour of the melody. The contour of a melody is its shape. A melody with a conjunct contour would move mostly in one direction by steps whereas a melody with a disjunct contour would move in many directions by different skips and leaps. A conjunct melody is easier to sing than a disjunct melody.

This Familiar Melody Moves in Skips

A Disjunct Melody

Leaps and Steps

leap   steps

Research indicates that contour is very important in the memory of a melody. Therefore, perception of the contour of melody is a first step in developing a conceptual understanding of melodies. Music educators provide young children with many experiences in interpreting the contour of melody. These experiences include interpreting the contour through body movement, drawing the contours of melodies, following the already drawn contours of melodies, and following the notation of familiar songs as they are performed. Older children might follow musical scores to compositions.

Drawing the Contour of Twinkle Twinkle Little Star

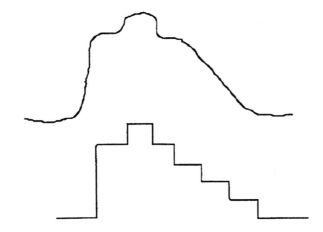

The Rhythm and Contour of Twinkle

The Notation of Twinkle

Twin-kle twin-kle   lit - tle star   How I won-der   what you are

Melodic Patterns and Tonality

As children improve in their melodic perception, music educators direct the children's attention toward the actual pitches and the patterns they form. "Movable do" is a pitch syllable system to aid the perception and singing of tonal patterns. It is a verbal association system very much like those used to aid the memory of rhythm patterns. Word syllables are used to represent pitches and their relationship to one another. For example, the two pitches represented by *sol mi* form a pattern that has a characteristic sound.

"Rain, rain go away" is an example of the *sol mi* pattern which naturally occurs in early childhood chant and song. Children often use *sol mi* when calling "mommy," or "daddy." Many music educators begin their tonal perception training with the *sol mi* pattern and other tonal patterns common to early childhood music. *Mi re do* (*Hot Cross Buns* or *Three Blind Mice*) is another common melodic pattern for early childhood.

sol   mi

Rain rain   go   a - way

The perception of pitch patterns leads to the development of the concept of tonality. Tonality is the concept that melodies are usually constructed from a particular arrangement of tones called scales. A melody will be constructed from the tones of a scale and have certain recurring tones which give the melody a feeling of resolution and finality. The following example is a familiar tune and its scale.

Major Tonality

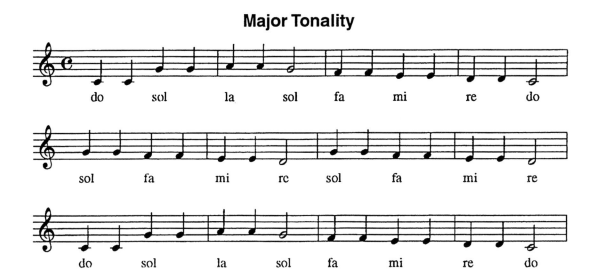

The Major Scale

do re mi fa sol la ti do

Notice the tones that occur frequently and the last tone of the tune. *Do* and *sol* are dominant throughout and the tune ends on *do*. In this instance, *do* is the home tone or tonic. This tune is based upon the major scale which gives it a major tonality.

There are many categories of scales in music and each has a distinct sound according to its arrangement of pitches. The major scale has the characteristic sound of *do re mi fa sol la ti do* and the minor scale has the characteristic sound of *la ti do re mi fa sol la*. The following tune is based upon the minor scale. Notice the predominance of *la* and *mi* and that the tune ends on *la*. *La* is the home tone. This gives the tune a minor tonality.

Minor Tonality

The Minor Scale

la   ti   do   re   mi   fa   sol   la

Two other scales that occur frequently are the pentatonic scale which has the characteristic sound of *do re mi sol la do* and the chromatic scale which is made up of half steps (all the pitches on the keyboard). Many folk songs and songs in early childhood are based upon the pentatonic scale; however, very few songs in elementary school are based upon the chromatic scale. The chromatic scale was very popular as a tonal source for art music during the 19th century. The following example illustrates the pentatonic and chromatic scales.

The F Pentatonic Scale

do   re   mi   sol   la   do

The Chromatic Scale

Reading Melody

Another important step in learning to perceive melody is the development of an aural sense of music notation. This is gradually achieved through many of the activities that were discussed earlier. Students develop an aural perception of melodic patterns and then associate this perception with notation. During this process the identification of the pitch syllables of notated patterns becomes very important. A student must know which note is *do* (sometimes *sol* is identified) to identify the other pitches and the characteristic sounds of the patterns that they form. Music educators often use guidelines like the following to aid labeling of pitch patterns.

"If *sol* is on a line, *mi* is on the line below"

"If *sol* is on a space, *mi* is on the space below"

As they gain in experience students learn that the key signatures (the #s or *b* s at the beginning of a piece of music) of songs identify the tonal function of the individual pitches of a song. For example, one flat (*b*) indicates that *do* is F whereas one sharp (#) indicates that *do* is G. Once *do* is determined, the students can identify the remaining pitches of a song.

Melody Summary

Melodies are groups of tones that are perceived as a whole. The major percepts of melody are that pitches are high and low, melodies have shape or contour, and melodies are usually constructed from scales which give them tonality. Music educators utilize body movement and a number of activities to aid children in their perception of high and low and the contour of melodies. The contour of the melody is one of the most important aspects of remembering melodies. As children develop their melodic perceptual skills music educators direct the children's awareness toward the actual pitch patterns. "Movable do" is a verbal association system used to remember the characteristic sounds of pitch patterns and to attach aural meaning to written melodic patterns. An aural sense of written music is an important outcome of the study of melody.

Goals and Objectives for Melody in the Elementary School

The students will discriminate between high and low pitches

The students will interpret melodic direction through body movement

The students will discriminate between steps, skips, and leaps in melodic movement

The students will discriminate between conjunct and disjunct contours of melodies

While listening or singing the students will follow and identify graphic representations of the contour of melodies

While listening or singing the students will follow and identify the written notation for melody

The students will identify familiar tonal patterns in melodies

The students will sing and perform with instruments familiar melodic patterns from notation

The students will discriminate between major and minor scales

The students will begin to distinguish between major and minor tonalities in melodies

Class Activities

1. Find and classify songs as to their overall contour. How do they move, by steps, skips, or leaps? Are they conjunct or disjunct?

2. Practice and memorize the characteristic sounds of the most common melodic patterns in elementary music. Use "movable do" to learn the following patterns: *sol mi, sol la sol mi, mi re do, do re mi, do mi, do re mi sol, do mi sol, do ti la, la do mi,* and *mi sol la.* Associate these patterns with their notation.

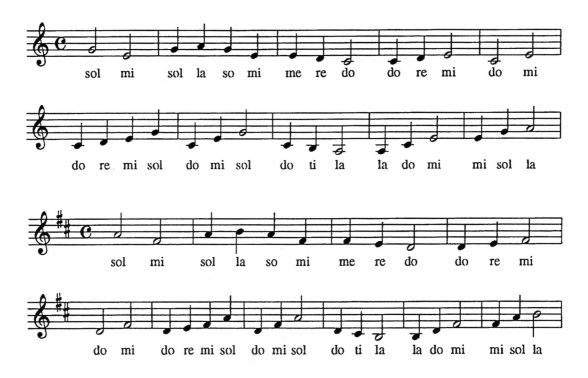

3. Practice singing the major and minor scales. (*do re mi fa sol la ti do* and *la ti do re mi fa sol la*)

4. Practice identifying pitch syllables, patterns, and tonalities from the notation of elementary songs. Learn to sing familiar songs from notation. For example, the first pitch syllable is given in each of the following familiar songs. Can you identify the remaining pitch syllables? Sing the songs with pitch syllables and identify the names of the songs.

5. Identify and compare the dominant melodic patterns (*mi la, do ti la*, etc.) of major and minor tunes. For example, compare the melodic patterns of *Rocky Mountain* and *Hey Ho Nobody Home* (see Folk Song Appendix).

HARMONY

So far the horizontal dimension of music has been discussed. Melody and rhythm go across the page as music is performed. The vertical dimension of music is called the texture of music. Harmony is a texture of more than one pitch sounded simultaneously. (One pitch sounding alone is called unison.) There are two basic harmonic textures in music, polyphonic (also called contrapuntal) and homophonic (or chordal). Music is polyphonic when one hears more than one melody at the same time. During certain periods of music history, polyphonic music was the dominant music performed and composed. As music evolved composers began to become aware of vertical sounds and the idea of composing from this vertical aspect led to homophonic or chordal music. This was the beginning of the use of harmony as an element in the composition of music. Melodies were written with a chordal accompaniment.

Polyphonic Texture

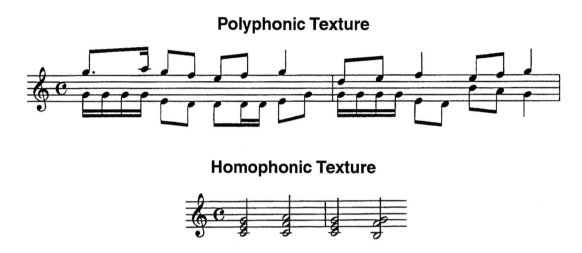

Homophonic Texture

Harmonic Perception and Performance

The perception of harmony evolves much later in the musical development of children than the perception of the other elements of music. The combination of tones forms a complex array of sounds that is difficult for young children to perceive. To develop a foundation for the perception of harmony and to foster the ability to sing in harmony, music educators use a variety of techniques. These involve the rhythmic and melodic *ostinato*, singing rounds, singing partner songs, and singing songs with *descants*.

An *ostinato* is a repeated pattern in music. Many instances occur when a music educator utilizes *ostinato* technique. A teacher might have part of the children chant "tick tock tick tock, ding ding ding ding" to accompany the singing of *Are you Sleeping*, or perhaps "bake that bread" to accompany *Pease Porridge Hot*. As the children become more skilled, they can begin to sing rounds and begin to use melodic *ostinatos* to accompany familiar songs.

Ostinato Technique

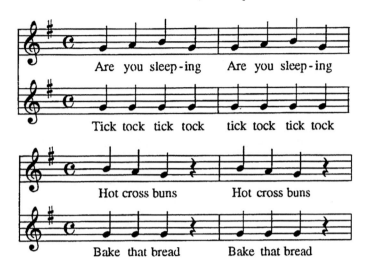

Partner songs are independent songs that can be sung together. *Merrily We Roll Along* and *London Bridge* will work as partner songs. *Three Blind Mice* and *Are You Sleeping* may also be sung as partner songs. Songs with *descants* have a second melodic line that compliments the primary melody. Often the second melody is higher than the original melody. Partner songs and *descants* develop performance independence and heighten student perception of harmony. Eventually, the use of *ostinato* technique, rounds, partner songs, and songs with *descants* develops the ability of students to sing in harmony and perceive harmony in music.

Partner Songs

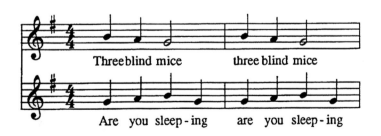

Familiar Song with Descant

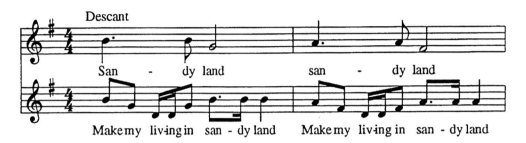

Chords, Intervals, and Triads

Developing a perception of harmony also includes the use of the auto-harp, xylophones, and other instruments that can perform chords. A chord is three or more tones that are sounded together. In elementary music, chords most often occur in the form of triads. A triad is a three tone chord built in intervals of a third.

Intervals

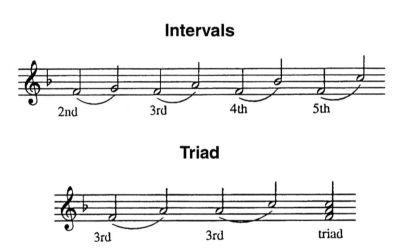

Chords and triads are like scales in that they also help establish a feeling of tonality. In elementary school, music educators deal primarily with major and minor triads. As in the scale discussion, a major triad can be thought of as being built upon *do. Do mi sol* illustrates the characteristic sound of a major triad. A minor triad can be thought of as being built on *la*. It has the characteristic sound of *la do mi*.

Major and Minor Triads

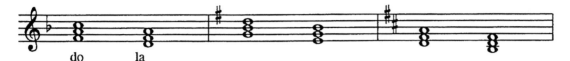

do   la

As elementary students' perceptual skills increase they learn to sing triads (major and minor), to identify major and minor triads, and to identify when the harmony or chordal accompaniment changes in a song. Most often the harmonic accompaniment utilizes only one or two chords and it is a relatively simple task to have the children identify when the accompaniment changes. The teacher may ask the children to raise their hands when they hear the harmony change or the teacher may strum the beginning chord of a song (while singing the song) and ask the children to tell when the harmony should change. The students can identify when the melody does not "fit" or "go with" the harmony.

The Autoharp

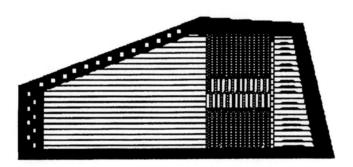

The autoharp is easy enough to play so that a student can strum the strings while the teacher presses the chord buttons. Xylophones can also be arranged so that children can perform chords with mallets, and there are different kinds of electronic keyboards that may be programmed to accompany many of the songs in elementary school. In most instances the chords are identified in the music of the song for accompaniment purposes.

Music with Chords Labeled for Accompaniment

Harmony Summary

Harmony is the vertical dimension of music which concerns the combination of tones. Music educators use *ostinato* techniques, rounds, partner songs, and songs with *descants* to develop harmonic perception and performance skill. An important aspect of harmony is the harmonic movement among triads and chords to accompany melody and establish tonality.

Goals and Objectives for Harmony in the Elementary School

Students will be able to perform chants and songs with rhythmic and melodic *ostinatos*

Students will be able to discriminate between harmony and unison music

Students will be able to sing rounds, partner songs, and songs with *descants*

Students will identify harmonic change in the accompaniment of one and two chord songs

Students will accompany one and two chord songs with the autoharp and other chord playing instruments

Students will be able to sing major and minor triads

Students will begin to discriminate between major and minor triads

Students will begin to discriminate between polyphonic and homophonic music

Class Activities

1. Practice adding rhythmic and melodic *ostinatos* to chants and elementary level songs. What *ostinatos* can you use with *Hickory Dickory Dock*, *Jack and Jill*, or *Jack Jumped Over the Candle Stick*?

2. Learn and practice rounds, partner songs, and songs with *descants*.

3. Practice singing the major and minor triads (*do mi sol* & *la do mi*).

4. Practice singing and accompanying songs with the autoharp. The following songs may be accompanied with only one or two chords. *Eency Weency Spider, Are You Sleeping, Hey Ho Nobody Home, London Bridge, Shoo Fly Don't Bother Me, Skip to My Lou*

FORM IN MUSIC

All music has form. Form is the internal and external design of music. It is how music is put together and organized. If music did not have form, a design, or plan, it would be very difficult to remember or even be perceived as music. Random sounds are not perceived as music because they do not have form.

Form in music ranges from the very simple form of a children's tune to the very complex forms of contemporary symphonies and operas. The more complex musical form becomes the more difficult the music is to perceive and understand. The ability to listen to music and perceive the design of that music is an important perceptual skill. It increases one's aesthetic reaction to music. Many authorities in music education and philosophy believe that the ability to perceive design in music is the key to musical understanding and aesthetic response to music.

The Primary Elements of Form

Balance, unity, and variety are the primary elements of form and design in music. Repetition is the basic means for achieving balance and unity. Musical ideas must be repeated in order to be remembered. One could almost say that repetition is a dominant element in music. Very seldom do we hear music that does not make extensive use of repetition. Often a whole piece of music may be based on one rhythmic or melodic idea. This is especially true in popular music. It is also true for many "great" classical works. Listen to the beginning of Beethoven's *Fifth Symphony* for example.

Variety is created by variation, change, and new ideas. Variety brings relief from the repetition. It surprises listeners and keeps their interest. If there is too much variety in music, the design is difficult to perceive and the music has less meaning to the listener. Some philosophers believe that the aesthetic response to music is caused by shifts between the repetition of ideas and the introduction of new ones. This interaction between repetition and variation is often very subtle and not obvious to the novice listener. However, as was mentioned previously, the more one is able to perceive, the more heightened will be the aesthetic reaction to music. Thus, in keeping with the goal of aesthetic sensitivity, one outcome of music education should be the ability to perceive form and design in music.

Same and Different Phrases

A beginning point in the perception of form with young children is the perception of repetition. The music teacher asks the children if the music is the same or different. "Are you sleeping, are you sleeping" is the same idea repeated. Is "Brother John, brother John," the same or different from "Are you sleeping?"

Same & Different

Another key element of form is the concept of phrases. Music occurs in complete musical thoughts known as phrases. The ends of phrases are often perceived as resting places in the melody and they are often marked by phrase lines. In performance groups, one learns to breathe only at the beginning and end of phrases.

Twinkle Twinkle Little Star

Phrases usually occur in pairs much like questions and answers. In *Twinkle Twinkle Little Star*, "Twinkle twinkle little star" could be perceived as a question phrase with "How I wonder what you are" being the answer phrase. Often the question phrase ends on *sol* and the answer phrase ends on *do*. This movement from *sol* to *do* is often called a cadence. It gives the two phrases a feeling of completion and direction.

Binary and Ternary Form

Phrases that work together are often combined with similar phrases to form sections. In elementary songs these sections may be identified as the verse and chorus (or refrain). To help children identify these sections, music teachers often label them as A and B sections and identify the music as two part (A B) form. In *Yankee Doodle* the first two phrases fit together to form the verse. If the verse is labeled A, the chorus, which is different, may be labeled B. Thus, *Yankee Doodle* is in binary (two part) form. Ternary form (three part) occurs when the song ends with the A section (ABA). *Twinkle Twinkle Little Star* is in ternary form.

Yankee Doodle

Most songs in elementary school are in binary or ternary form. There are a number of different activities that help develop a perception of form. Identifying "same and different" has already been mentioned as one technique. Another is called "turning the phrase." Music teachers lead the children in identifying phrases by using arm movements to signify phrase length. The children change arms and movement directions when the phrases change in the music. Another "turn the phrase" technique is to walk one direction for one phrase and change directions when a new phrase begins. Another technique is to have children stand on a "question phrase" and sit on the "answer phrase." Many music teachers have children improvise answer phrases to question phrases sung by the teacher. The teacher might improvise "What do you like to eat?" on *sol* and *mi* and individual children answer on *sol mi do* or *mi re do* to give the feeling of cadence and completion.

Question and Answer Phrases

Children may also use movement to identify different sections of a song. Many times teachers have children diagram the sections of a song using circles and triangles or other geometric shapes.

Ternary Form

Music teachers also use *ostinato* technique to develop formal concepts. Young children may chant "tick tock tick tock ding ding ding ding" as an *introduction* and *coda* (a special ending) to *Are You Sleeping*.

Are You Sleeping

Introduction (2X)	Tune	Coda (2X)
"tick tock tick tock ding ding ding ding"	"Are you sleeping"	"tick tock tick tock ding ding ding ding"
A	B	A

Since the *introduction* and *coda* are the same in this example, the arrangement could also be considered as ABA or ternary form.

Other Forms

Another form that is not so common in elementary music is called *rondo* form. This form is characterized by a repeated section occurring between contrasting sections as in ABACA. In this example, A appears between the contrasting sections of B and C. At certain times during music history the *rondo* was a very popular form in classical music. The fourth movement of Mozart's *Eine Kleine Nachtmusik* is a famous classical *rondo*. The *rondo* form is not common in popular music or elementary music; however, music teachers often lead children to develop their own *rondo* forms in creative activities. A "train rondo" might be created by combining the following train songs and chants.

A Train Rondo

Arranged by Arlene Herndon

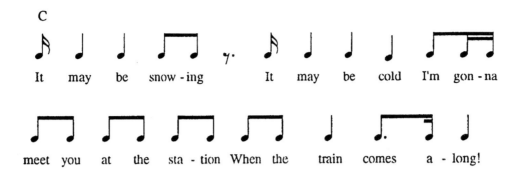

Perform in ABACA Rondo Form

Another form that is common in "classical music" is the theme and variation. The theme is a melody which is followed by variations on that melody. This form might be diagramed as A A' A" A'" A"". Each variation is based upon the original melody or harmony but changed or varied in some way. The composer may change the rhythm of the melody, tonality, harmony, or even change the pitches and contour of the melody. Sometimes the harmony is the only retained element of the theme. Jazz is a form of this type of theme and variation. The jazz musician plays the theme and then improvises a melody over the harmony of the theme. There are many famous theme and variations written by our greatest composers. *Variations on a Shaker Theme* from *Appalachian Spring* by Aaron Copland is a famous theme and variations. *The Young Person's Guide to the Orchestra* by Benjamin Britten is a good example of a theme and variations.

Form Summary

Form is the internal and external design of music. It plays an important part in our perception of music. Form is created by the repetition and contrast of musical ideas. This often subtle interaction between repetition and contrast contributes to the aesthetic reaction to music. The perception of form in music is an important outcome of music education.

Music educators use a variety of techniques to lead children to discover same and different patterns in music, question and answer phrases, and to label binary and ternary song forms. Two other important forms in music education are the *rondo* and the theme and variations.

Goals and Objectives for Form in the Elementary School

The students will be able to distinguish between same and different patterns (melodic and rhythmic)

The students will be able to identify phrases aurally and through body movement (turn the phrase)

The students will be able to identify same and different phrases

The students will improvise vocally and instrumentally question and answer phrases (*Do - sol, sol - do*)

The students will be able to identify same and different sections aurally and through body movement

The students will label and diagram binary and ternary song forms

The students will demonstrate a knowledge of theme and variations form by identifying and discussing techniques of variation

Students will diagram and create simple *rondo* forms

Class Activities

1. Practice identifying the form of such popular elementary songs as *Kookaburra, Chatter with the Angels, A Ram Sam Sam*, and others. (See Folk Song Appendix)

2. Practice improvising question and answer phrases. Use the following procedure. Sing "What do you like to eat" as the question patterns. Sing "I like ——" as the answer patterns. Gradually add variety to your questions and answers until you are improvising question and answer phrases.

3. Listen to Aaron Copland's *Appalachian Springs - Variations on A Shaker Tune* and discuss the ways Copland achieved variation.

4. Create and perform a "Rain" *rondo*. Find rain songs and chants and combine them into a "Rain" *rondo*.

TIMBRE

Timbre in music is often referred to as the "tone color" of the sounds that are making the music. Different instruments and voices have characteristic sounds which the listener recognizes in music. Manipulating the timbre of the music is one way composers create expression in music. Consider the difference in expression that would be created by different instruments playing a familiar tune. A tuba playing *Merrily We Roll Along* will create a very different effect from a violin playing the same tune. Of course, in music the listener usually hears many different and similar timbres performed simultaneously. Imagine all the different sounds that are possible when a symphony orchestra and a large chorus perform together. The perception of timbre is a very important element in the aesthetic response to music.

The perception of timbre is one of the earliest perceptual skills and interests that children develop. Almost from the very beginning of life children respond to different sounds. Some believe that the fetus in the womb even recognizes and reacts to different sounds. Thus, the exploration and discovery of different sounds is an important part of the natural development of young children.

Exploring Sound

Music teachers often lead children in various activities to explore and discover the different sounds that different objects and instruments can make. These activities might include exploring the sounds created by different sized containers filled with water or the different sounds that can be created by different sized "homemade" rhythm instruments or drums. Students may also experiment with the effects of length on the sound of vibrating strings.

As students explore and discover different timbres they may be led to discuss the principles of sound production. These principles are that sound is caused by vibration and that the sounds of objects are affected by the materials they are made of and by how the sounds are produced. An object sounds differently according to whether you strike it, rub it, or pluck it. The size, length, and density of the object also affect the sound. Small objects sound "high" and big and hollow objects generally sound "low." Short objects sound "higher" than longer objects.

Children also experiment with the different timbres of their classroom musical instruments. A wide range of tone colors and textures are possible with tambourines, hand drums, xylophones, glockenspiels, autoharps, and other classroom instruments. Students may explore the sounds of these instruments by creating sound compositions and special effects for poems and short story dramatizations.

Exploring Instrumental Sounds

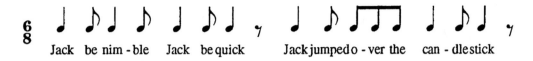

On each "Jack" play the hand drum. On the rhyming works "quick" and "stick" play the bells or a triangle. On "over the" play a *glissando* up on the mallet instruments.

Explore Your Voice

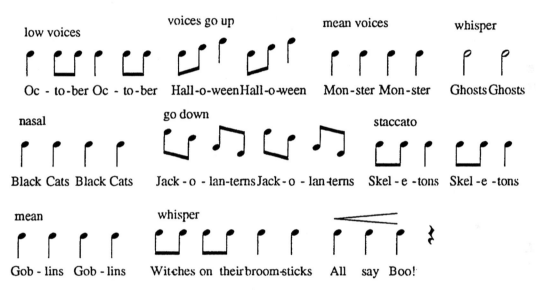

After exploring your voice, transfer vocal sounds to body percussion (stamp, pat, clap, snap)

The Instruments of the Orchestra

As children begin to understand the principles of sound production they are introduced to the instruments of the orchestra. This may be done through orchestral music like *Peter and the Wolf* by Prokofiev, *The Young Person's Guide to the Orchestra* by Britten, or other works that feature contrast in timbre as a primary focal point of the music. As children learn to identify the sound of different orchestral instruments they are shown pictures of the instruments and taught how the sounds are produced on the instruments.

On woodwind instruments, sounds are generally produced by blowing air across a reed on a mouthpiece. Vibrating the reed causes the tone to be produced. This is true for all the woodwind instruments except flute. The clarinet and saxophone are reed woodwind instruments. On the flute, the vibrations are created by blowing the air over the aperture (mouthpiece opening) of the flute. The air stream is actually split by the edge of the mouthpiece opening. This split causes the vibration which produces the tone on the flute. Some woodwind instruments use double reeds (two reeds tied together) to produce the tone. The oboe and bassoon are double reed instruments.

Sounds are produced on brass instruments by vibrating or buzzing the lips into the mouthpiece. This vibrates the air stream and produces the tone. Common brass instruments are the trumpet, French horn, trombone, and tuba. Percussion instruments create sound when they are struck. Striking the drum, a mallet instrument, or the cymbals causes vibration and produces tone. Tones are produced in the string family by two techniques. Bowing the string (*arco*) causes vibration and tone and plucking (*pizzicato*) the string also produces tone. The violin, viola, cello, and bass are the instruments of the orchestra string family.

Changing the pitches on the instruments of the orchestra is achieved by changing the length of the tubing of the instruments. The more finger holes on a clarinet that are covered makes the tubing longer. Therefore, as more holes are covered the pitch is lowered. The length in tubing on brass instruments is controlled by valves and slides. Pressing certain valves on the trumpet or moving the slide on the trombone changes the tubing and the resulting pitch. The lower sounding percussion instruments are larger or longer. The bars that produce low notes on the xylophone are longer than the bars that produce higher tones. String length on the string instruments is controlled by pressing the string to the instrument. This shortens the length of the string that vibrates from the bow and changes the pitch.

Electronic and Vocal Timbres

A rather new type of instrument is the electronic instrument and the digital synthesizer. These instruments are capable of producing a wide range of tone colors. In fact, some instruments called samplers reproduce the actual sounds of other instruments. This makes it possible for the musician and composer to perform a wider range of "real tone colors" from a keyboard. Many contemporary recordings of popular music utilize these instruments. These instruments are often operated with a computer. The computer sends electronic signals to the digital synthesizer which tell the synthesizer what tone colors and music to produce.

Another important timbre in music making is the vocal timbre. Male, female, and children's voices are often heard in music, especially choral music, and they are capable of a wide range of vocal textures. One usually thinks of soprano, alto, tenor, and bass as the primary voice timbres and ranges; however, there are many others. Baritone (between tenor and bass), *mezzo* soprano (between alto and soprano), and *coloratura* soprano (very high opera voice) are also common voice timbres.

Timbre Summary

Timbre is the tone color or "quality" of the sounds produced by instruments and voices in making music. The timbre of instruments is affected by the materials that instruments are made of and by how the sounds are produced (striking, plucking, etc.) Timbre is perceived by children almost from the very beginning of life. Children should be led to explore and discover different timbres in their environment and in music. Learning to identify the instruments of the orchestra and different voice classifications is an important part of perceiving music.

Goals and Objectives for Timbre in the Elementary School

Students will explore and discover timbres in their classrooms and environment

Students will recognize the characteristic sounds of simple classroom instruments like bells, the tambourine, and rhythm sticks

Students will identify the characteristic sounds of the instruments of the orchestra

Students will demonstrate a knowledge of how the sounds are produced on the different instruments of the orchestra

Students will use different timbres and sound effects to dramatize poems and stories

Students will discuss the expressive effect of the use of different timbres in music

Class Activities

1. Utilize classroom percussion instruments and pitched instruments to dramatize limericks and stories. For example, add instruments for sound effects to *Hickory Dickory Dock* or *Jack and Jill*. Also see *The Wind* in Chapter Five.

2. Explore the sounds of classroom instruments and materials through the creation of sound compositions. Some suggestive titles might be "hurricane," "the playground," or "the shore."

3. Listen to orchestral works such as the *Young Person's Guide to the Orchestra* by Benjamin Britten, *Peter and the Wolf* by Prokofiev, and *Pictures at an Exhibition* by Mussorgsky. Discuss the expressive effects created by the different instrumental timbres.

EXPRESSION IN MUSIC

The previous sections of this chapter have discussed what are commonly referred to as the elements of music: rhythm, melody, harmony, form, and timbre. Another element of music, in fact, the most important element of music is the expression that music creates. This emotional expression is created by manipulating the elements of music that have already been discussed. Therefore, if one can perceive the elements of music and how the composer has used them, one's aesthetic reaction to the music is enhanced. This supports the theory of "teaching the perception of the elements of music" which was discussed in Chapter 1.

One obvious way that a composer creates expression is in the performance directions of a piece. These directions most often are about the tempo (speed) of the music, the dynamics (volume), or the style (accented or smooth). It is easy to understand how performance directions affect the expression of music. A funeral march would not sound like a funeral march if it were played fast, loud, and accented. Thus, a musically educated person must understand the musical terms and definitions that instruct the performer in creating expression. The following list represents but a few of the many musical terms and definitions that describe how the music is to be performed.

Musical Performance Directions

Tempo		Dynamics		
Largo	broad, large	*pp*	*pianissimo*	very soft
Lento	slow	*p*	*piano*	soft
Adagio	leisurely	*mp*	*mezzo piano*	moderately soft
Andante	flowing	*mf*	*mezzo forte*	moderately loud
Moderato	moderate	*forte*	*f*	loud
Allegretto	lively	*fortissimo*	*ff*	very loud
Allegro	rapid, fast	*crescendo*	*cresc.*	gradually louder

| *Vivace* | quick | *decrescendo* | *decresc.* | gradually softer |
| *Presto* | very fast | *diminuendo* | *dim.* | gradually softer |

| *accelerando* | gradually faster |
| *ritardando* | gradually slower |

The combination of different rhythm patterns, the contour and tonalities of melody, the harmonic movement of chords, the repetition and variety of form, and contrasts in timbre all affect the expression of music. Music educators help students identify expressive devices and the effects they create through a variety of techniques. Children may interpret the characteristic rhythmic feeling of a composition through movement or emphasize the rise and fall of the contour of a melody through their singing. Often they listen to music and discuss what expressive effects were created by such techniques as repetition, sudden contrasts, modulation (changing tonalities), *accelerando*, and *crescendo*.

Expression Summary

Expression in music is created by the composer's manipulation of the elements of music. This includes the performance directions of a piece as well as the composition of the music itself. As students' skills in perceiving the elements of music increase, their reactions to the expression in music are heightened. This leads to aesthetic experiences with music and increased aesthetic sensitivity.

Goals and Objectives for Expression in the Elementary School

Students will interpret the characteristic rhythmic feeling of music through expressive body movement

Students will sing with expressive attention to phrase length and melodic contour

Students will discriminate between different tempos and dynamics

Students will identify changes in tempo and dynamics

Students will discuss the effects created by such techniques as *accelerando, ritardando, crescendo,* and *diminuendo*

Students will compare and contrast different percepts of rhythm, melody, harmony, form, and timbre in relationship to the effects they create in music

Class Activities

1. Experiment with the expression of familiar melodies by changing their rhythm patterns and tonalities. For example, sing *Twinkle* in minor or in triple meter. Use syncopation or dotted rhythms to change the effect of *Mary Had a Little Lamb*.

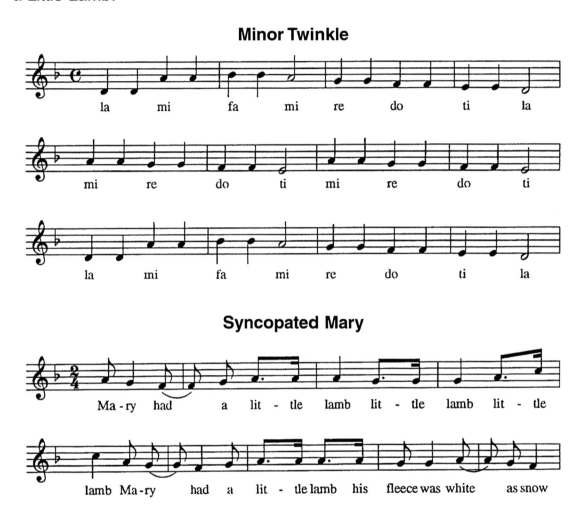

Minor Twinkle

la   mi   fa   mi   re   do   ti   la

mi   re   do   ti   mi   re   do   ti

la   mi   fa   mi   re   do   ti   la

Syncopated Mary

Ma-ry had   a   lit - tle   lamb   lit - tle   lamb   lit - tle

lamb Ma-ry   had   a   lit - tle lamb   his   fleece was white   as snow

2. Listen to selected examples of recorded classical and popular music and identify the techniques composers utilized to create expression. Some very good listening guides for this purpose are available in *Ear Bending* and the *Pop Hits Listening Guides* by Michael Bennett from Pop Hits Publications, Memphis, Tenn. Recommended selections are *Variations on a Shaker Tune* from *Appalachian Spring* by Aaron Copland and the pop tune *Flowers are Red* by Harry Chapin.

CHAPTER SUMMARY

This chapter has discussed the major elements of music as they are presented in elementary music education programs. These elements are rhythm, melody, harmony, form, timbre, and expression. Movement, singing, and verbal association systems are important means for aiding children in their perception of these elements. As children become more skilled in their perception of the elements of music, the more enhanced are their aesthetic experiences with music.

The following are the elements of music and the underlying percepts that are taught in most elementary school music programs.

Rhythm	Melody	Harmony	Form
pulse	high & low	ostinato technique	same & different
accent	contour	rounds	phrases
meter	patterns	partner songs	sections
duration	scales	descants	binary
patterns	tonality	changing harmony	ternary
		major &	rondo
		minor triads	theme & variation

Timbre
explore sounds
principles of sound
classroom instruments
orchestral instruments
voices, electronic instruments

Expression is created by the composer's manipulation of these elements through performance directions, dynamic levels, and compositional techniques.

SUGGESTED RESOURCES

Bennett, M. D. (1977). *Ear bending: Twelve on and off beat guides to classical listening.* 3149 Southern Ave., Memphis, TN.: Pop Hits Publications.

Bennett, M. D. (1977). *Pop hits listening guides.* 3149 Southern Ave., Memphis, TN.: Pop Hits Publications.

Machlis, J. (1984). *The enjoyment of music,* (5th ed.). New York: W. W. Norton & Company, Inc.

Chapter 3

CHILD DEVELOPMENT AND PRINCIPLES FOR LEARNING MUSIC

An important part of understanding music education and being able to use music in the education environment is understanding how children develop musically. Just as a classroom teacher must be able to prescribe specific language arts activities for certain age levels or developmental stages, so should a teacher be able to determine appropriate music activities for different aged children.

It is obvious even to the casual observer that children go through different developmental stages in music. Young children cannot do some things that older children find easy to do with music. Young children may have difficulty clapping the rhythm pattern of melodies whereas older children find clapping melodies easy. Older children can sing in harmony; younger children may not sing in tune. Research in the area of child development in music has revealed some general sequences of musical development that children experience. It appears that stages of development occur both in music perception and performance.

For many years an important question in musical development has been the "nature versus nurture" argument. Are children born musical or do they develop musicality because of environmental influences? Most psychologists today would agree that children are born with musical ability, or as Harvard psychologist Howard Gardner has claimed, musical intelligence (Gardner, 1983). Certainly some children possess more musical intelligence than others just as some children are better at math or language arts than others. However, every one is born with musical intelligence, and with the proper environment, everyone can develop musical skills. So the answer to the "nature versus nurture" question in music is "both." Genetic heritage does influence musical development but the environment also plays a crucial if not critical role.

Music psychologist Edwin Gordon has identified a developmental aptitude in music. His research indicates that children have a developmental aptitude for music which seems to level off at about age nine. He suggests that early musical experiences are critical for the full development of this music aptitude (Gordon, 1984).

PERCEPTUAL DEVELOPMENT AND CONCEPT FORMATION

As a reference point for perceptual development and concept formation in music, consider the first three stages of child development outlined by the developmental psychologist Piaget (Flavell,1963). Piaget believed that children go through progressive stages of mental ability and that the first developmental stage of children is dominated by the senses. This stage, the sensorimotor, occurs from birth to about age two. The child's world consists of what is seen, touched, heard, and the senses of taste, hunger, and movement. During this stage the child may perceive and identify sounds by loudness, timbre, and pitch.

Musical experiences for children in the sensorimotor stage should be dominated by sensory experience. A variety of musical sounds and styles should be played for the sensorimotor child. Different timbres, textures, and the rocking motion that often accompanies lullabies stimulate the child's aural and movement senses and form a foundation for later learning and interest in music.

According to Piaget, the next stage of development occurs from about age 3 to 7. During this stage, the preoperational stage, language develops and the child can begin to use icons (symbols) to aid perception and concept formation. The preoperational stage may be a critical age for musical development. As Gordon and others have found, musical aptitude (some say natural musical development) appears to level off after the preoperational stage.

The child is able to perceive more during the preoperational stage but perception and concept formation are still influenced very much by the kinesthetic and visual senses. Musical experience during the preoperational stage should include many movement experiences, a variety of dynamics and tempos, and utilize visual aides and body movement to facilitate the formation of musical concepts. During this stage, children are apt to focus on one thing at a time and music seems to exist in opposites rather than on a continuum. Thus, tempo is slow or fast, dynamics are loud or soft, sounds may be long or short, and pitch is high or low. Musical concepts appear to develop in the following sequence from the sensorimotor through the preoperational stage.

dynamics (loud and soft)
timbre
tempo (slow and fast)
duration (long and short)
pitch (high and low)

By the end of the preoperational stage, children should be able to recognize loud and soft, different instruments, fast and slow, simple rhythm patterns, high and low pitches, simple pitch patterns and melodic contours. A tremendous amount of musical growth can occur during the preoperational stage.

The sensorimotor and preoperational stages are critical periods for the development of musical concepts. During these stages children develop what psychologists call "schema" for music. These schema are models or formulas for the characteristics of music. These formulas are the foundation for the development of musical perception and response.

Piaget's third stage of development is called the stage of concrete operations. During this period, which occurs from about 7 to 12, children are able to perform more complex mental operations. They become able to decenter attention and action. They are able to reverse thoughts, sequence events, place musical concepts on a continuum, and transfer learning. They are apt to be able to perform *ostinatos*, rounds, and to perform with instruments to accompany their singing. They become able to do more than one thing at a time. The period of concrete operations occurs from about the second through the sixth grades.

During this period children develop the ability to perform the mental operation of conservation in music. This is the ability to recognize that certain properties of music (for example the melody) may stay the same even though other properties (the rhythm or timbre) have changed. This is a very important mental process in music perception. It leads to the perception of form and greater understanding in music. As was mentioned previously, the subtle interaction between repetition and variety in music is very important to the aesthetic response. As children develop the ability to conserve, the more enhanced are their perceptions of the interactions between repetition and variation in music.

In recent years, many psychologists have begun to question Piaget's developmental stages. It appears that specific domains of learning, culture, and instruction all may influence developmental stages (Flavell, 1985). It is interesting to note, however, that the more recent theories on child development are very much related to Piaget's theory. (Hargreaves and

Zimmerman, 1992). Piaget's stages of development still seem applicable as a general framework or guide to child development.

Gardner (1973) has criticized Piaget's stages because their end result is scientific or logical thought. He argues that development in the arts does not necessarily lead to scientific and logical reasoning. For example, intuition, creativity, and novel thinking may not be accounted for in Piaget's stages of development. Gardner believes that artistic development occurs along three paths that eventually interact and work together. These paths are those of the maker (creator, performer), the perceiver, (critic), and the feeler (audience member). To Gardner artistic development occurs mostly between the ages of 2 and 7 when the child begins to use symbols. Interestingly, Gardner's symbolic development coincides with Piaget's preoperation stage. Gardner, Piaget, and other psychologists generally agree that children do begin to process information differently around the ages of 5 to 7, the period that coincides with the end of the preoperation stage and Gardner's development of symbol use.

THE DEVELOPMENT OF PERFORMANCE SKILL

As mentioned previously, it is rather obvious that children go through different stages in their performance of music. Older children may move easily with the pulse of the music whereas younger children find it very difficult to coordinate their movements to the pulse. Second graders may sing "rounds" but kindergarten children may have difficulty singing on pitch. Research indicates that performance skill in music, movement and singing, are both developmental and influenced by experience.

Music psychologist Edwin Gordon has identified a "musical babble" stage which all children seem to pass through. Music "babble" seems to begin during the sensorimotor stage and continue through the first years of the preoperational stage. This "babble" is much like the speech "babble" that children go through in learning language. Children babble vocally before they sing and they babble physically in their movement response to music (Gordon, 1984).

Music "babble" is characterized by an exploratory response to music. The child experiments with vocal sounds, pitch gliding, and spontaneous song. The child moves to music, but in an unstructured manner. Gordon emphasizes that informal, not structured, musical experiences are the preferred mode of music experience during the "musical babble" stage. Children emerge from the "babble" stage when they can sing phrases on pitch and echo chant rhythms. Then they are ready for more structured experiences with music.

Gordon believes that movement to music during the babble stage is critical for the child's development of movement skill and rhythmic response to music. This movement may be simply swaying, rocking, or moving like animals; the important criterion is that the child move to music. Once a child starts to repeat movements to music and attempts to coordinate movements to the pulse, the child is ready to chant rhythm patterns and pat to the pulse of the music. The development of an accurate kinesthetic response to music is long range, however. Children require many experiences in chanting and movement to the pulse before they are able to coordinate their movements to the pulse.

Singing during the babble stage is essentially experimentation with vocal inflection and sing song chant. There is not a tonality or definite pitch to this exploratory singing. During this period, the child should be sung to often, although it is not necessary that the child sing on pitch or learn the melody of the song. As in movement, it is important that the child just experience singing. Once the child starts repeating tones and singing melodies around a single tone, the child is beginning to hear pitch centers and to develop a sense of tonality. Then the child can match pitch for part of a song and sing simple patterns like *sol mi.* As they sing and hear more songs, young children are able to approximate the contour of songs and eventually develop the ability to sing in tune throughout the song. It is critical, however, that children be sung to and attempt to sing many songs in different tonalities and meters.

McDonald and Simons (1989) have synthesized the research findings reported by child developmentalists in the following age referenced singing characteristics. These characteristics are observed from the sensorimotor stage through the pre-operational. They also follow the pattern of what Gordon has called singing "babble."

Age Referenced Singing Characteristics

Age	Characteristics
12-18 months	Vocal play experimentation with sound.
19 months	Melodic and rhythm patterns appearing in vocalizations
19-24 months	Free experimentation with songs; short spontaneous songs, often consisting of a small melodic interval with flexible rhythm patterns.

2 years	Use of melodic pattern from learned songs in spontaneous singing. Ability to sing parts of songs.
21/2-3 years	Imitation of songs, though rarely with total accuracy.
4 years	Sequence followed in learning songs: words, rhythm, phrases, melodic "contour."
5-51/2 years	Sense of "key" stabilized; can sing most songs when learned fairly accurately.

Adapted from Davidson, Mckernon, and Gardner, 1981 (McDonald & Simons, 1989, page 46).

FOSTERING THE DEVELOPMENT OF MOVEMENT SKILL

The development of movement skill is very important to the future development of music sensitivity. There are a number of activities and techniques that the teacher, day care administrator, or music educator can do to foster this development.

First, there should be many opportunities for movement to music. With the very young child these opportunities include free response, creative movement, finger plays, and simple singing games. For free response and creative movement, the teacher might play a recording or the piano and ask the children to move the way the music feels. With young children, the teacher may model movement at the beginning. The teacher might ask, "Can you sway the way I can, or how can you move your arms?" Once the child sees a model, they usually create movements for themselves. Moving like different kinds of animals, trees in the wind, and clouds in the sky are good suggestions for young children's movement activities.

The music itself may suggest a certain movement. Music educators often use songs in compound meter (6/8) to suggest skipping to the beat. For example, *The Mulberry Bush* is a good skipping tune. Simple duple meter songs often suggest marching. Children may hop to some songs and gallop to fast compound meter tunes. Music teachers may improvise these different meter patterns on the hand drum or the piano to indicate the type of movement for the children. The following patterns suggest marching versus skipping.

Marching

Skipping

The 3/4 meter can suggest long steps with a sway.

As children learn to move to the hand drum or piano, the teacher may have them "freeze" when there is silence. Another signal for "freeze" might be a different timbre such as a recorder playing. Teachers often use signals during movement activities. They are good for teaching aural perception and following directions.

Children can also do expressive movements to poems, rhymes, and fingerplays as part of the development of their movement skill.

Five Little Pumpkins

Five little pumpkins sitting on a gate, (hold up five fingers)
The first one said, "Oh my, it's getting late!" (one finger, dramatize)
The second one said, "There are witches in the air!" (two fingers, make
    flying motions)
The third one said, "But I don't care!" (three fingers, shrug hands)
The fourth one said, "Let's go and have some fun!" (four fingers, excited)
The fifth one said, "Let's run, run, run, run, run!" (five fingers, running)
Then "Oooo" went the wind, and out went the light, (bring hands down gradually, close
    eyes)
And the five little pumpkins rolled out of sight. (rolling motions with hands)

(Adapted from Staton, Staton, Davidson, & Snyder, 1988, p. 46)

Wee Willie Winkie

Wee Willie Winkie,
Runs through the town, (fingers run)
Upstairs and downstairs, (fingers climb up and down)
In his nightgown,
Rapping at the window, (knocking motion with fist)
Crying through the lock, (hands around mouth)
Are the children in their beds,
For now it's eight o'clock.

Expressive rather that accurate movements are the focus of these types of activities. Movement in early childhood is a process rather than a product. The goal is to develop movement skill and rhythmic sensitivity to music.

Action songs and singing games are also good means for the development of movement skill. *The Wheels on the Bus, Johnny Pounds with One Hammer,* and *Clap Clap Clap Your Hands* are action songs. The words of the songs suggest action by the singers.

The Wheels on the Bus

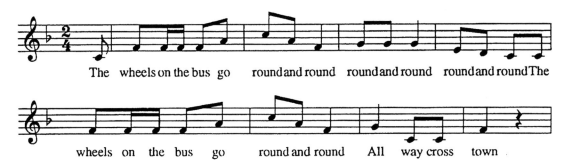

The wheels on the bus go round and round round and round round and round The
wheels on the bus go round and round All way cross town

Johnny Pounds with One Hammer

John - ny pounds with one ham - mer one ham - mer one ham - mer
John - ny pounds with one ham - mer then he pounds with two

Clap Your Hands

Clap clap   clap your hands   Clap your hands to - ge - ther   Clap clap

clap   your   hands   Clap   your   hands   to - ge - ther

Singing games involve group activities and group coordination. Very young children may have difficulty performing singing games, but these games are very attractive to children who are mature enough to do the various steps and body movements. Many authorities believe that singing games should begin with circle games which gradually develop in complexity to line games and folk dances. Circle games may include acting out games, imitation games, choosing partner, and chase games. As children mature they can perform line games with arches, double circle games, and square dances.

A Circle Game

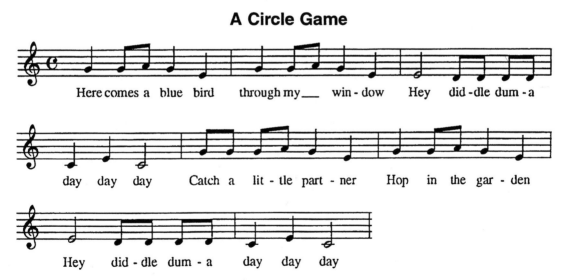

Here comes a blue bird   through my___ win - dow   Hey   did - dle dum - a

day day day   Catch a lit - tle part - ner   Hop   in the gar - den

Hey   did - dle dum - a   day day day

In a circle children hold hands up high to make windows. The child who is the bluebird flies like a bird in and out the windows. On "Catch a little partner," the bluebird chooses someone and they hold hands facing to "Hop in the garden" (the circle). The partner is now the new bluebird.

Rhythmic Sensitivity

As children continue to develop their motor and rhythmic skills it is very important that they practice moving accurately to the beat. As mentioned previously, with young children, the easiest coordination with the beat is to chant. "Ta ta ta ta" or "du du du du" may be used to practice feeling the beat. Simple patting movements are also easy for the young child. Young children can pat both hands downward on their thighs (a bilateral movement) with more pulse accuracy than by clapping their hands together. Generally, bilateral movements are easier for young children to match to the pulse. Clapping and stepping to the pulse are not bilateral. Stepping accurately to the pulse is probably the most difficult of muscle movements to the pulse for the young child.

Movement and dance specialist, Phyllis Weikart, has developed a four step language process for the development of rhythmic sensitivity. The first step of this process is chant, or "Say." The child chants a body part, for example, "head head head head." The next step is "Say and do." The child chants and taps the head lightly with both hands. The third step is "Whisper and do." The child whispers and taps. The fourth step is "Think and do." Weikart believes this process should be done without music first. Then, as the children are able to identify the pulse of recorded music, the process should begin with "Whisper and do" to music.

Weikart begins with bilateral tapping on one body part, then alternating tapping on one body part, followed by combinations of bilateral tapping on two body parts (head and shoulders). Clapping and stamping to the music are attempted after the children are able to tap the pulse with simple bilateral and alternating movements. Weikart emphasizes that these first experiences in rhythmic competency should be attempted while seated so that the problem of balance does not complicate coordination with the pulse (Weikart, 1989).

Weikart's Four Step Process

Say (chant "head head head head")
Say and do (chant "head" and tap head lightly with both hands)
Whisper and do (Whisper "head" and tap head lightly with both hands)
Think and do (tap head lightly with both hands)

As children are able to pat to the pulse of the beat they should begin practicing echo chanting rhythm patterns. The teacher may use recorded music or perform on the piano music that has a very definite pulse feeling without a rhythmically complex melody. The children pat (both hands downward on the thighs) to the pulse and echo rhythm patterns chanted by the teacher. For example, while maintaining the pulse with the class the teacher chants "ta ta ti ti ta" and the children echo on the pulse immediately by chanting "ta ta ti ti ta." After the children are able to keep the pulse and chant patterns the teacher may show the rhythm patterns in "stick" or regular notation on the chalk board or with flash cards.

THE DEVELOPMENT OF SINGING SKILL

The development of singing skill in young children is very critical to their overall perceptual development and aesthetic response to music. Although there are some natural aspects to the development of singing, there are some very important experiences that must occur for children to develop their singing skills to their fullest potential. As mentioned previously, it is extremely important that the very young child be sung to often and that the child experiment with and attempt to sing a variety of songs.

Pitch Matching Games

The parent or teacher must sing often with the child and practice echo singing and pitch matching games. These activities should be informal and "fun" with accuracy not being the criteria for success. As in movement, the development of singing skill is gradual and occurs over the years from the sensorimotor stage through the preoperational stage. However, singing experiences are critical during these developmental stages.

Can you sing into my microphone? (holds make believe microphone)

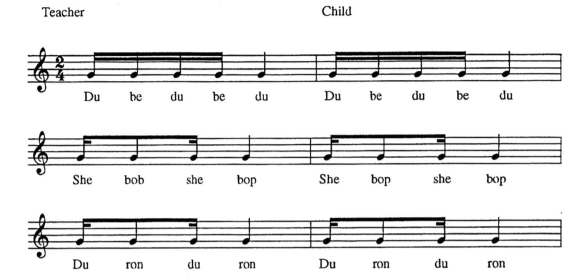

As McDonald and Simons (1989) have summarized, the singing skills of children appear to develop in the following sequence. Children are first able to learn the words and accompanying rhythms of favorite songs, next they are able to approximate the contours of songs and repeat single phrases (for example "e i e i oh" from *Old MacDonald*), then they are able to sing complete songs in tune. To encourage this development music teachers supplement early singing experiences with chant and expressive speech activities.

Jack and Jill

Jack and Jill went up the hill (pitch from low to high)
To fetch a pail of water (carry the pail with a swing)
Slosh, slosh,slosh, slosh
Jack fell down! (high to low skip in pitch)
crash - boom!
And Jill came tumbling after (High to low)
Flump flump flump flump! (roll hands and arms)
Drip drop drip drop (gradually slower and softer)

This is accomplished with limericks, rhymes, and poems or with finger plays. Music educators use the voice dramatically to illustrate feelings and characters in poems and stories. They lead the children to experiment with voice inflection to develop the perception of high and low.

Principles for Teaching Singing

Some important principles of teaching singing have been expressed by the Kodaly practitioners of music education. The Kodaly method focuses on the development of singing skill.

1. Sing many songs with the "sol mi" pattern. Many believe that all children learn to sing the "sol mi" pattern first as in the familiar childhood chant "rain rain go away." Research does indicate that children do sing in a small range and do sing descending patterns first. Whether are not the "sol mi" pattern is a natural development of singing skill or whether it is a culturally induced phenomenon is not clear. But, children do seem to sing the "sol mi" pattern easily and there are many songs with this pattern that are appropriate for early childhood music.

2. Teach the difference between speech sounds and singing. All too often young children tend to "shout" rather than sing. This "shout" comes from the chest or throat rather than the "head." According to singing experts, young children should be taught the differences between a speaking voice (chest or throat voice) and the singing voice (the head voice). The low speaking voice range is very constricted and hard to control. Young children find it easier to match pitches in their head voice. The head voice should have a "light airy tone."

Teachers may lead the children in "siren" or "whistle" exercises to find their proper singing voices. They may also play "Simon Sings" with the children. The children must listen carefully to "Simon" (the teacher) give directions. If the teacher sings, the children are to follow the direction (touch your toes), if the teacher speaks, the children remain stationary.

3. Sing softly, slowly and clearly. Emphasize singing softly with a "good sound." Children can hear one another and sing in tune more accurately if they sing in a soft light voice. It is also better for their voices to sing softly. When they sing loudly, children tend to shout from their chest voices as mentioned above. Shouting can be harmful to further development of the voice. Sing slowly and distinctly. Many times, teachers will sing songs too fast for the children to perceive the words or the melody. Slow the tempo down, the tempo can be increased later.

4. The very young child (three and four years old) may not sing with others in a group. They may sing alone, however. Provide many opportunities to sing alone and with a group.

5. Choose songs with a small range (an interval of a fifth or sixth). Young children (preschool and kindergarten) do not have a broad or a particularly high range. They are most comfortable singing songs with limited ranges that center between middle C and the A above on the keyboard.

Older children (second grade and older) may expand their singing range to include an octave or more.

6. Sing without accompaniment at first. Singing without accompaniment makes it easier for the children to perceive the melody and match the pitch. Children should have many opportunities to listen to the teacher and to other children sing without accompaniment. When accompaniment is used (autoharp, piano, or guitar) it should be simple enough not to interfere with perception of the melody.

7. The teacher must be able to sing songs in the appropriate keys with good intonation. In early childhood, music is learned primarily through imitation. The children must have good models of singing. It is very important that the teacher be able to demonstrate singing on pitch, with good voice quality, and expression.

Selecting Songs for Young Children

Most songs sung by young children are major and in duple meter. Songs in minor and triple meter are rare; therefore, children may find them difficult. When possible, however, children should have the opportunity to sing a variety of songs in different meters and tonalities

The teacher should choose songs that are age appropriate and songs that relate to the children's particular environment. Popular music songs and themes are not appropriate for teaching singing to young children. Some other factors to consider when choosing songs for young children are the length of the song, the amount of repetition in the song, the text of the song, and the musical complexity of the song.

Songs for very young children should generally be short with frequent repetition. Dialogue songs, songs with echo response, and songs with repeating parts are excellent for the younger child. The text of the songs should flow easily with the melody and be age appropriate.

When considering the musical complexity of a song, the range, contour, and rhythm patterns are very important. In most instances the range should not exceed an octave, the contour should be mostly conjunct with very few large leaps (particularly upward leaps), and the rhythms should be easily perceived and coincide with the text. Even syncopation is easily performed if properly matched with the text. For example "Shoo fly don't bother me" is a very complex rhythm that is easily performed because of the text.

Teaching a New Song

Once a teacher has selected an appropriate song for the students, there are definite procedures to consider in teaching the song. Songs for early childhood and elementary school are often called "rote" songs. Rote songs are simple (short) songs often of folk origin that are easily taught to young children by imitation. The teacher should consider the following steps in presenting the "rote" song to students.

Many believe that the students should be motivated to learn the new song; thus, the teacher usually discusses aspects of the song that might motivate the students to listen to the presentation and to learn the song. For example, the teacher might say. "Today, we're are going to learn a song about a rabbit who had a bad habit. What was this rabbit's bad habit? You tell me after listening to the song." More than likely, young children will be motivated to listen to a song about a rabbit because the teacher has given them a specific question to answer upon hearing the song.

Next, the teacher sings the song through slowly and distinctly. In *John the Rabbit* the children can sing the "O Yeah" parts on the first presentation. The teacher might say, "Sing 'O Yeah' with me when I point to you." After the first presentation, the children answer the motivation question and the teacher may elaborate by asking further questions about John's activities. "What did John do in the garden and what did he eat?"

John the Rabbit

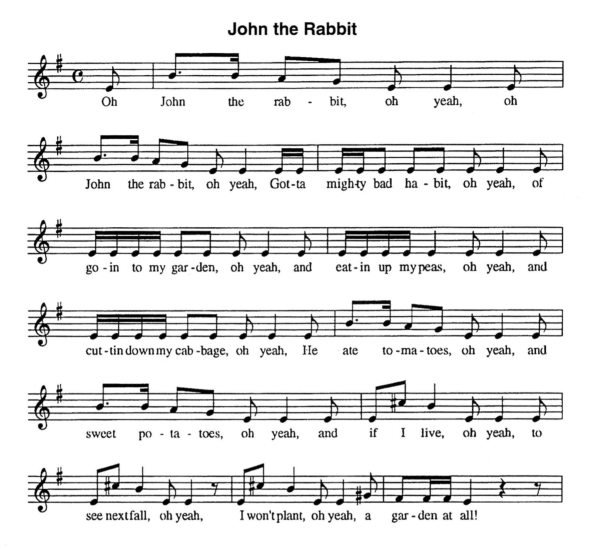

Oh John the rab - bit, oh yeah, oh

John the rab - bit, oh yeah, Got-ta migh-ty bad ha - bit, oh yeah, of

go - in to my gar -den, oh yeah, and eat-in up my peas, oh yeah, and

cut-tin down my cab -bage, oh yeah, He ate to -ma -toes, oh yeah, and

sweet po - ta - toes, oh yeah, and if I live, oh yeah, to

see next fall, oh yeah, I won't plant, oh yeah, a gar - den at all!

Next the teacher simply asks the children to sing along. The teacher should give the starting tone and a beginning gesture like "Here's your pitch - oooh, ready sing." As the children attempt to sing the whole song the teacher can identify sections that are difficult for them. The teacher may isolate these sections after the children have had an attempt at the whole song.

Learning a new song is a gradual process. The "whole contour" of the song will be remembered before specific pitch patterns. Thus, children should be made conscious of the contour of the melody. This can be achieved with arm movements or whole body movements. Singing on pitch throughout the whole tune develops gradually.

The children should have many attempts at singing a song over a period of time. Once they have learned a song, the children will want to sing it often and the teacher may use it in a variety of ways. The text may be changed to integrate the song with other subjects or the teacher may teach a movement game to accompany the song.

MUSICAL EXPERIENCES FOR EARLY CHILDHOOD

As indicated previously, the most important aspect of music in early childhood is experience. Infants and young children should have a wide variety of experiences with music. Parents and day care providers should sing and chant to infants and imitate their vocalizations. For example, the day care provider may use a singing voice to give instructions to young children or as an accompaniment to routine activities. "Lets go wash our hands" may be sung in a *sol mi* pattern or "That's a good girl" (or boy) might be sung to the infant while feeding them. When infants "coo" and "babble" adults may echo them. This will delight the infant and become the foundation for pitch matching games and singing.

Infants may be rocked to the pulse while being sung to or rocked to the pulse of appropriate recorded music. An adult may take hold of the infant's arms and move them (lightly) in time to the pulse, or pat the infant's hands with the pulse. Adults may hold infants and dance to music or move the child to rhythm patterns and melodic direction.

Two and three year old children sing naturally while they play. Adults should encourage this improvised singing with comments such as "Sally I really like your doll song," or "Billy, your truck song is very nice." Group singing activities may be utilized with this age but adults should be aware that group singing may not be on pitch and that children often have different vocal ranges which inhibit their success in singing with a group. Very often children who will not sing in a group may be heard singing familiar songs individually as they play.

Free movement to appropriate recordings throughout the day should be encouraged and as the children develop, adults may make them aware of fast and slow, smooth versus jumpy, and other characteristics of tempo and rhythm in music. But again, the emphasis should be on free and improvised movement. Movement recordings by Hap Palmer, Raffi, and Greg and Steve work very well for two, three, and four year old children.

Another important element of early childhood music should be opportunities to explore the sounds of rhythm instruments and other natural instruments (pots and pans) in the early childhood environment. Children enjoy closing their eyes and identifying the sounds of different instruments and objects in the classroom. They enjoy creating rhythm bands to accompany chants, movement, or just for fun.

Music in early childhood should be a natural part of the child's day with emphases on exploring, discovering, and free improvised singing and movement. With singing and movement as a natural element in their environment, young children will develop into musically sensitive individuals.

GUIDELINES FOR SINGING AND MOVING IN THE ELEMENTARY SCHOOL

The child's singing and moving skills develop gradually over the elementary years. Kindergarten children are just beginning to sing on pitch, second graders may be using melodic ostinatos and singing very simple rounds, and fourth graders may sing partner songs and accompany their singing with instruments. The kindergarten child enjoys fingerplays and free movement to music, the second grader can participate in circle games, and the fourth grader is beginning to learn folk and square dance. Some classes will have more advanced musical skills than others. However, the following are some general guidelines and examples that the classroom teacher may use for singing and moving in the elementary school.

Grades K-1

Singing - begin with chant and sol mi songs, songs should have a small range (c to a) and move mostly in steps and skips (*Teddy Bear*, Pease Porridge**)
Movement - finger plays (K), chant pulse, pat pulse, free movement, stepping, skipping, hopping, simple singing games (*Bow Wow Wow*, Ring Around the Rosie, and Bluebird**)

Grades 2-3

Singing - larger range (octave), still conjunct songs (steps and skips in mostly same direction), use *ostinatos* (chant, body percussion, and simple melodic), very simple rounds (*Kookaburra*, Who's That**)
Movement - imitation singing games and games that require keeping the pulse, more complex circle games (*Punchinella*, Circle Round Zero**)

Grades 4-5

Singing - octave or better range, rounds, partner songs, more complex contour (*Hey Ho Nobody's Home*, Hear Ye The Wind Is Rising**)
Movement - more complex games (*John Kanaka**), beginning folk and square dance

* see Folk Song Appendix

THE DEVELOPMENT OF MUSIC PREFERENCE

Another developmental aspect of music learning is the development of musical preferences. During the sensorimotor stage and the early years of the preoperational stage, children like and respond positively to all music styles. The one deciding factor concerning preference during these early stages is tempo. Children overwhelmingly prefer faster music. This preference for faster tempos continues throughout childhood until early adolescence.

As early as five years old, the child starts to prefer popular music to other musics. There are a number of reasons for this phenomena. Popular music is heard throughout the day on radio and television, and the child's immediate peers and older models express preference for the popular music styles. Television commercials for children even use popular music style. Popular music style is the dominant music style in society, therefore, most prefer it to others. One goal of music education is that people be open to and actually prefer styles other than popular music. There is much aesthetic reward to be gained from a variety of music styles - jazz, folk and ethnic music, and of course, classical. How can teachers influence young children's preferences so that they will listen to all styles of music? The following are a few principles that will foster broader preferences for all musics.

1. Play a variety of musics for children. The overriding factor in not liking or learning from something is familiarity. Most children do not hear any music other than pop and church music. Children should have the opportunity to hear folk and ethnic music, jazz, and the various styles of classical music.

2. Play music that is fast and predominantly instrumental. Children do not like slow music or the operatic voice style. Introduce vocal music gradually at fast tempos in nonoperatic styles. Choral music would probably be preferred to single voice solos.

3. Use good equipment and good recordings. The quality of the sound is very important in preference decisions.

4. Model preference for art or "classical" music. "Boys and girls isn't this Mozart just wonderful?" Research indicates that young children will imitate the preferences and attitudes of older authority figures.

5. Repetition. Play a variety of musics often, but be sure to repeat selections. After hearing a Mozart piece two or three times, children will begin to respond to its melodies. These repetitions may be as background music, or music to accompany other activities. Teachers do not need to play popular music, however. The students are already familiar with it.

PRINCIPLES FOR LEARNING MUSIC

The previous discussions indicate that child development in music is a gradual process with a critical period for music experience occurring during early childhood. Children gradually develop music perceptual skills from dynamics and timbre through melody, form, and harmony. Singing and movement skill also develop gradually over the early childhood years. During these early childhood years it is very important that the child experience a wide variety of singing and movement to music activities. These activities form a framework for later musical learning.

As music psychologists have observed the development of children in music, certain principles for learning music have been developed. The following are some of these principles for learning music.

Modeling, Imitation, Verbal Association, and Symbolic Association

Music is learned in much the same way as language, through imitation. Language is heard and spoken before written symbols are used to represent sound. In learning music, children must first hear music and then sing. In fact, the aural model is the most effective means for presenting music to children. Music psychologist Edwin Gordon has named this first stage of learning aural/oral. As children hear and imitate music in early childhood and beyond, music educators use verbal association to aide the memory and perception of the characteristic sounds of patterns. This verbal association may be rhythm syllables or the "movable do" system discussed in Chapter Two.

After the imitation and verbal association stages, written symbols are utilized to represent familiar patterns of rhythm and pitch. Learning written symbols (notation) is a gradual process as in language and occurs over a number of years. As in language, notation for familiar patterns (words and phrases in language) is learned first.

Whole Part Whole

Music is perceived in wholes not isolated units. Remember that a melody is a group of tones perceived as a whole. Therefore, when learning unfamiliar music, children should first experience the whole. After the whole has been experienced then the song may be presented in phrases (small wholes).

Contour

At first children remember the contour of melodies rather than specific pitch patterns, therefore, music teachers draw children's attention to the contour when presenting unfamiliar music. This may be accomplished with whole body movement, hand or arm movement, or graphic representation.

Visual Aides and Body Movement

During early childhood, the senses play an important role in learning. Thus music educators utilize visual aides and body movement to enhance music learning experiences. Visual cues may be hand signs or graphic representation (arrows or lines to represent contour). Movement may involve rocking, patting, and clapping the pulse, expressive movement, or movement to interpret contour, phrases, or musical form.

Familiarity

Perhaps the most important principle of learning music is that students learn from the familiar. Children must learn many songs to build their music vocabulary. They must first recognize patterns before they can discriminate between patterns. A lack of familiarity may be the reason children do not learn to value classical or art music. Unfamiliar music does not have meaning for young children.

CHAPTER SUMMARY

Children go through stages of musical development both in what they perceive in music and in how they perform music. The sensorimotor, preoperational, and concrete operation are important stages in the musical development of children.

Children form musical concepts according to the following sequence: dynamics, timbre, tempo, duration, and pitch. The development of rhythmic and singing skill is a gradual process with musical experience playing a key role in this development. Children should be sung to and experience movement to music often. They should experience a variety of tonalities, meters, and styles. These experiences form "mental schema" which become the foundation for musical learning.

Chanting to the pulse of music with "bilateral" movements such as patting is suggested as a means for developing rhythmic skill. Pitch matching games, learning the difference between "singing" and "speaking" voices, and the proper vocal range for young children are important considerations in the development of singing skill. Musical preferences can be influenced by informal exposure to music, modeling, and by the use of music with fast tempos. Music is primarily learned through imitation. As children develop they may learn to associate words and word syllables to familiar patterns of music. After this verbal association stage, children may learn music notation. Learning music notation, however, is a gradual process, and develops over a number of years.

Children should initially experience unfamiliar music as a whole. The contour of the melody of unfamiliar music is an important first perception. Visual cues and body movement are important means for aiding the perception of contour, pulse, and patterns in early childhood.

The familiarity of music is probably the most important aspect of music for the development of perceptual skills and musical preferences. Young children should become familiar with a wide variety of music.

Class Activities

1. Visit a day care center and observe the children in music activities. Can you distinguish different stages of musical development among the children?

2. Practice and learn pitch matching games like those given at the beginning of this chapter. Can you create your own?

3. Use voice inflection and body movement to dramatize early childhood rhymes, limericks, and stories. For example, create a dramatic presentation of *Three Billy Goats Gruff* or *The Three Bears*.

4. Observe the rhythmic development of young children. Compare the rhythm abilities of preschool, primary, and upper elementary age children. Compare their abilities to clap patterns and tap a steady beat.

5. Try Weikart's four stage language process for movement activities to develop a feel for the pulse of music.

6. Practice some early childhood singing games like *Here Comes a Bluebird* and *Punchinella*. (See Folk Song Appendix) Also see Choksy, L. & Brummitt, D. (1987) *120 Singing Games and Dances for Elementary Schools*. Englewood Cliffs, NJ : Prentice-Hall, Inc.

7. Observe music classes in early childhood. Are the children singing in their head voices and in the appropriate range? What techniques does the music teacher use to teach proper singing?

8. Peruse the music text book series and other song sources for songs appropriate for early childhood, the primary grades, and upper elementary school. What differences in musical complexity and vocal range do you observe between songs designated for these age groups? For example, what are the differences between *Bow Wow Wow* and *Hear Ye the Wind is Rising*?

Bow Wow Wow

Hear Ye the Wind Is Rising

9. Select some songs appropriate for early childhood and the primary grades. Outline and practice a sequence for teaching them according to the principles suggested in this chapter.

SUGGESTED RESOURCES

Boswell, J. (Ed.). (1985). *The young child and music: Contemporary principles in child development and music education: Proceedings of the music in early childhood conference.* Reston, VA: Music Educators National Conference.

Choksy, L. (1981). *The Kodaly context: Creating an environment for musical learning.* Englewood Cliffs, NJ: Prentice-Hall, Inc.

Choksy, L. & Brummitt, D. (1987) *120 Singing Games and Dances for Elementary Schools* . Englewood Cliffs, NJ. : Prentice-Hall, Inc.

Flavell, J. H. (1963). *The developmental psychology of Jean Piaget.* New York: Van Nostrand Reinhold Company.

Flavell, J. H. (1985). *Cognitive development* (2nd ed.). Englewood Cliffs, NJ: Prentice-Hall Inc.

Gardner. H. (1973). *The arts and human development.* New York: John Wiley & Sons.

Gardner, H. Davidson, L. & McKernon, P. (1979). The acquisition of song: A developmental approach. *National symposium on the applications of psychology to the teaching and learning of music.* Reston, VA: Music Educators National Conference.

Gardner, H. (1983). *Frames of mind.* New York: Basic Books.

Gordon, E. E. (1984). *Learning sequences in music.* Chicago: G.I.A. Publications, Inc.

Hargreaves, D. J., & Zimmerman, M. P. (1992). Developmental theories of music learning. In R. Colwell (Ed.), *Handbook of research on music teaching and learning.* New York: Schirmer Books. (pp. 377-391).

Mark, M.M. (1986). *Contemporary music education* (2nd ed.). New York: Schirmer Books.

McDonald, D. T., & Simons, G. M. (1989). *Musical growth and development, birth through six.* New York: Schirmer Books.

Staton, B., Staton, M., Davidson, M., & Snyder, S. (1988). *Music and you, Grade 1, Teacher's Edition.* New York: Macmillan Publishing Company.

Weikart, P. S. (1989). *Teaching movement and dance.* (3rd ed.) Ypsilanti, MI: The High Scope Press.

Zimmerman, M. P. (1971). *Musical characteristics of children.* Reston, VA: Music Educators National Conference.

Chapter 4

CONTEMPORARY APPROACHES TO ELEMENTARY MUSIC EDUCATION

The most popular approaches to teaching music in the elementary schools today are the Kodaly method, the Orff process, and the music textbook series. Although methods by Emil St. Jacques Dalcroze, Edwin Gordon, Suzuki, and those who advocate the comprehensive musicianship philosophy are often mentioned in discussions about elementary music education, the dominant methods today are Kodaly, Orff, and the music textbook series. These methods are most often observed and presented at professional workshops and conferences. The Kodaly and Orff methods even have their own professional societies.

This chapter will present the basic premises and theories behind these methods to elementary music education. The reader will discover and learn much about contemporary music education through a basic understanding of Kodaly, Orff, and the textbook series. Most contemporary elementary music programs utilize some of the techniques and theories included in these methods for teaching elementary music.

THE KODALY METHOD

Zoltan Kodaly was a twentieth century Hungarian composer known primarily for his choral works and the music education method that is named after him. Kodaly believed that the human voice was the key to music education. He emphasized the development of music literacy through singing. Many music educators consider his approach a singing method; however, as the reader will discover, there is much more to Kodaly than singing.

Kodaly emphasized that children should study the folk songs of their culture. This idea was based upon the observation that just as children first learn their own language so should they first learn their own music. Thus, the content of the Kodaly method is determined by the culture of the community. In Hungary, Kodaly practitioners study Hungarian folk music; in America, they study the folk music of the particular region. The content of a Kodaly class in southern California will be different from that in southwest Virginia or urban New York.

Kodaly also believed that music education should follow the natural development of the child. This belief, along with the musical culture of the child, and the emphasis on singing, are the primary elements of the Kodaly method. Children study the folk songs of their culture as they progress through their natural developmental stages. Singing is the primary means of this study.

According to Kodaly authority Lois Choksy, Kodaly's basic philosophy of music education may be summarized by the following points.

> That music literacy is something everyone can and should enjoy
> That singing is the foundation of all music education
> That music education must begin with the very young
> That the folk songs of a child's own culture is his musical
>   mother-tongue and should be the vehicle for early instruction
> That only music of the highest artistic value (folk and composed) should be used in teaching

(Lois Choksy, *The Kodaly Context*, p. 11, Copyright 1981. Reprinted by permission of Prentice Hall, Englewood Cliffs, NJ.)

Characteristics of the Kodaly Method

The Kodaly method has some very obvious characteristics which are observable in most contemporary music classrooms. Perhaps the most obvious is the use of the Curwen hand signs to enhance the memory of tonal patterns. The Curwen hand signs are used with "movable do" in learning different patterns from the pitches of the pentatonic scale.

The Curwen Hand Signs

Sol   **Mi**

The sequence of the tonal patterns presented in the Kodaly method follow the natural abilities of children and the content of children's music. The first songs learned are based upon *sol mi*, sometimes called the natural interval. As discussed in Chapter Three, this interval is very easy for most children to sing, and many early childhood songs are based upon these two tones. *Peas Porridge Hot* and *Teddy Bear* are but two popular *sol mi* songs from early childhood.

The sequence of tonal patterns progresses until all the pitches of the pentatonic scale are included. Most Kodaly teachers introduce these pitches in the following sequence: *sol mi la do re*. After *sol mi* songs, the children sing songs with *sol mi* and *la*, then songs with *do* are added followed by songs with *re*. This practice adheres to cultural norms and child development principles. Folk music is often pentatonic and children are able to sing pentatonic music quite easily. After the children are skilled with pentatonic music, the other pitches, *fa* and *ti* are added to complete the diatonic scale (*do* to *do*).

A system of rhythm syllables is used to learn rhythm patterns. The most common rhythm syllables used by Kodaly teachers are based upon a system of *tas* and *ti tis* identified in Chapter Two. The rhythm sequence most often begins with *ta ta ta ta*, and then progresses to *ta ta ti ti ta* and *ta ti ti ta ta*. The following chart illustrates a very simplified sequence of melodic and rhythm patterns and the accompanying songs.

Sequence of Tonal and Rhythm Patterns

Melodic Pattern	**Rhythm Pattern**
sol mi	*ta ta ti ti ta*

Blue Bells

Melodic Pattern	**Rhythm Pattern**
sol la sol mi	*ti ti ti ti ti ti ti ti*

Acka Backa

Ac - ka bac - ka so - da crac - ka

Melodic Pattern	**Rhythm Pattern**
do	*ta ta ta rest*

Bow Wow Wow

mi re do   *ta ta ta rest*

so la so mi re do   ta ti ti ta ta

Other characteristics of the Kodaly method are reading and writing rhythm patterns with "stick notation," the use of *ostinato*, "inner hearing," and the "mystery song" technique. Stick notation and *ostinato* technique are described in Chapter Two. "Inner hearing" is a technique by which the teacher asks the children to "think" parts of a familiar song. For example, the teacher might ask the children to put the first phrases of the familiar song *Bow Bow Belinda* inside their heads and only sing the "Won't you be my darlin" phrase. This is done in tempo so that the children will sing together at the appropriate point. Inner hearing activities encourage the development of tonal and rhythmic memory which are very important to perceiving music.

Inner Hearing

(Think first three phrases, sing last phrase)

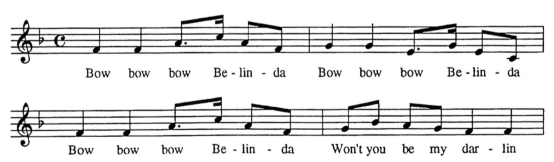

The use of "mystery songs" is a technique by which the teacher asks the children to identify a familiar song from its rhythm or primary melodic pattern. The song is one which the children have sung many times with words, hand signs, and rhythm syllables. In *Bow Bow Belinda* the teacher would clap the primary rhythm and ask who could identify the "mystery song." Notation is also used with "mystery song" activities.

Mystery Songs

(Belinda, Pease Porridge, Hot Cross Buns)

The Pedagogical Process

A very important component of the Kodaly method is its pedagogical process. The process is very systematic and organized. It is a valuable tool for organizing the content of elementary music education. There are four basic stages to organizing the learning activities in the Kodaly method. These stages are *prepare, make conscious, reinforce,* and *assess*. The content of the music curriculum (drawn from the child's culture and developmental stages) is presented in each stage.

In the *prepare* stage, the teacher prepares for the learning of a new melodic or rhythm pattern by singing many songs which contain the new pattern. These songs are learned by rote and may be accompanied by musical games or movement activities. The new pattern is not identified, the students just become familiar with it as part of a new song. This prepare stage may utilize a number of songs over a period of weeks.

In the *make conscious* stage, the teacher leads the children to discover the new pattern and to identify it by syllable and symbol. For example "Teddy Bear, Teddy Bear" would be made conscious as "*sol sol mi, sol sol mi.*"

During the *reinforce* stage the teacher leads the children to identify the pattern in their other familiar songs. The class practices singing the pattern with hand signs, placing the pattern on the staff, writing the pattern with stick notation, reading the pattern on the staff, flash cards and in familiar songs, and creating phrases and *ostinato* patterns with the pattern.

After the class demonstrates skill and confidence with the pattern, the *assess* stage involves identifying the pattern in unfamiliar songs and singing the pattern from notation in unfamiliar songs. The four stage process moves from the familiar to the unfamiliar and follows the basic principles of learning music discussed in Chapter Three. The learning activities that occur throughout the process are hearing, singing (aural/oral), deriving (verbal association), writing and reading (symbolic association), and creating.

As mentioned previously, the pedagogical process and cultural-child developmental philosophy of Kodaly are very efficient for organizing the content of elementary music education. The pedagogical process identifies learning activities of instruction while the children's culture and developmental stages identify when concepts are taught. This facilitates the organization of the wide variety of materials and activities which make up elementary music education. The following chart illustrates a very simplified version of how the Kodaly method contributes to organization and planning in elementary music. As can be seen, the teacher may prepare one pattern while making conscious, reinforcing, and assessing other patterns. Sample learning activities are given as the teaching of *sol mi do* is tracked through the chart.

Prepare	Make conscious	Reinforce	Assess
sing many songs with *sol mi do*	*mi do*	*do*	*la sol mi*
	Derive *sol mi do*, sing with hand signs, place on staff		
		Identify *sol mi do* in familiar songs, mystery song and inner hearing activities,	
			Read *sol mi do* from notation in unfamiliar song

hearing, singing, deriving, writing, reading, creating————————————

A Kodaly lesson in the elementary school will have many of the elements of the sample lesson given in Chapter One. Singing with hand signs, echo clapping, and movement are all components of a Kodaly lesson. Because of the Kodaly emphasis on vocal development, singing and singing games are the focus of the Kodaly lesson. This singing is almost always unaccompanied. Kodaly practitioners believe that accompaniment actually interferes with the young child's singing. Much emphasis is placed upon singing in the correct head voice, singing softly, accurately, and with musical expression. Choksy has suggested an outline for a Kodaly lesson which contains the following elements.

I. Greeting

Sung by teacher on melodic pattern most recently learned. For example "Hello, how are you" on *sol mi*. Children respond with "I am fine" on *sol mi*. The teacher then leads the class in hand singing the *sol mi* pattern.

II.   Opening Song

A familiar song with the *sol mi* pattern perhaps with an ostinato.

III.   New Rote Song

To prepare a new melodic or rhythm pattern.

IV.   Rhythm Skill Activity

Echo clapping, writing (dictation) a rhythm pattern, or reading a pattern on flash cards

V.   Movement, Singing Game or Dance

For example, "The Mulberry Bush"

VI.   Melodic Skill Activity

Deriving the notation of a familiar song through hand singing, placing the first phrase on a staff, or reading a new song from staff notation.

VII.   Familiar Song

Inner hearing exercise

VIII. Movement or Dance to a familiar song, or a song for listening sung by the teacher

(Adapted from Lois Choksy, *The Kodaly Context*, p. 172, Copyright 1981. Reprinted by permission of Prentice Hall, Englewood Cliffs, NJ.)

The Kodaly philosophy speaks of everyone's right to enjoy musical literacy. This should not be interpreted as just the reading and writing of music. Components of the Kodaly method are often used to teach sight singing (music reading) but in reality, the Kodaly method is a very comprehensive system of music education. Kodaly practitioners believe that true music literacy is not only the ability to read and write music but also the ability to perform, think, appreciate, and create music.

THE ORFF PROCESS

Carl Orff was a twentieth century German composer known for his compositions for chorus and orchestra and the music education process that bears his name. His most famous works are *Carmina Burana*, a staged oratorio for chorus and orchestra, and *Musik fur Kinder*, a series of pieces written for children's performance. It is from his "Music for Children" that the Orff process of music education has developed.

Characteristics of the Orff Process

Orff believed that music, speech, and movement are inseparable and that children should experience music as it evolved through history. Thus, his process of music education emphasizes speech (rhythmic and expressive chant) and movement. From the beginning children explore dramatic speech, chant, and movement which leads to what Orff called *elemental* music, or children's music.

Over a series of lessons, the Orff teacher will lead the children to explore and manipulate a musical idea until it evolves into what is often called a "set piece." This piece may utilize dancers, singers, dramatization, and instrumental performers.

Some characteristics of the Orff Process are similar to the Kodaly method. Orff practitioners utilize "movable do," the pentatonic scale, rhythm syllables, and many also use the Curwen hand signs for pitch perception. Orff differs from Kodaly in the use of the Orff Instrumentarium. The Orff music class has a wide variety of percussion instruments, recorders, and specially constructed glockenspiels, xylophones, and metallophones. Chant and movement are dominant characteristics, and the Orff teacher uses the *ostinato, introduction, coda*, and *bordun* to create form in the *elemental* music that evolves from the process discussed below.

Orff Instruments

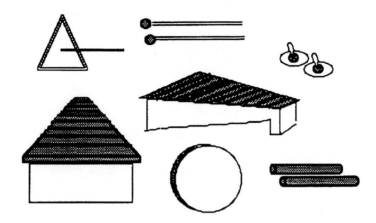

The Pedagogical Process

Unlike Kodaly, the Orff process does not have a systematic means of structuring the content of elementary music education. This is why Orff is usually referred to as a process rather than a method. It might be considered an approach to elementary music education rather than a systematic method. The basic components of this approach are Imitation, Guided Exploration, and Improvisation.

Imitation

This is the aural/oral stage of learning mentioned in Chapter 3. The teacher presents speech, movement, rhythmic, and melodic patterns to the students through modeling and imitation. Imitation may be simultaneous as in "do what I do." The teachers models a movement, dance step, rhythm pattern, or melodic pattern and the students imitate simultaneously. Remembered imitation occurs with echo clapping, singing, playing instruments, or moving, and overlapping imitation utilizes *canon* or round techniques.

Canon

Guided Exploration

The teacher leads the children to explore different possibilities and combinations of music concepts, ideas, and patterns. The children may be led to explore different combinations of rhythm patterns to use as an *ostinato* for a chant or they may experiment with different instruments to create tone colors to accompany dramatic speech and movement. The key component of guided exploration is that the children form musical concepts and skills through their own exploration, manipulation, and creativity.

Chant with Ostinato

Improvisation

After the children have developed skills and confidence with certain patterns and movements they are encouraged to improvise music and dance with these patterns and movements. The rhythmic *ostinato, bordun* (a harmonic *ostinato* on *do* and *sol*), and the pentatonic scale are used to set up a structure or accompaniment for improvisation.

In the following example, a teacher might use the chant *Hambone* with the accompanying "stamp clap" *ostinato* to develop an accurate rhythmic sense or "feel" for four beats. After the students have developed confidence with the chant and *ostinato*, the chant may be "left out" while individual students improvise rhythm patterns between class performances of the "stamp clap " *ostinato*.

Rhythmic Improvisation

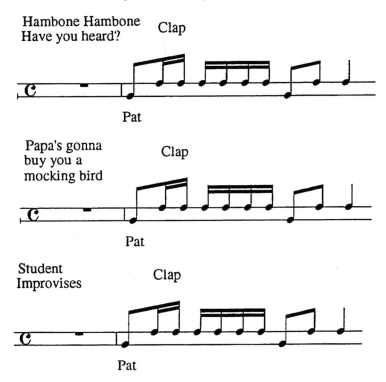

An Orff specialist might use a similar procedure with *Lil Liza Jane* and a *bordun* to create instrumental melodic improvisation opportunities for students. All the notes of the pentatonic scale "fit" or "sound good" with the *bordun*. Students would improvise with the mallet instruments of the Orff Instrumentarium.

Melodic Improvisation

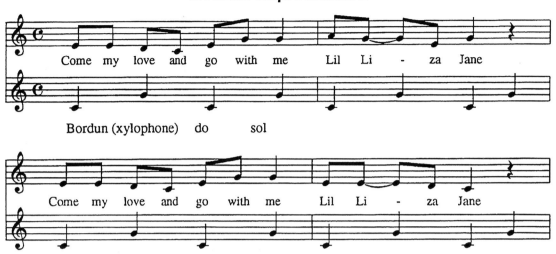

Goals of the Orff Process

According to Choksy, Abramson, Gillespie, and Woods (1986), the goals of the Orff process are the following:

1. sense of community
2. understanding of the organization of music
3. comprehension of music as an art
4. musical independence
5. personal musical growth
6. performance ability
7. self-esteem

(Choksy/Abramson/Gillespie/Woods, *Teaching Music in the Twentieth Century*, Copyright 1986, page 139. Reprinted by permission of Prentice Hall, Englewood Cliffs, NJ.)

These goals are readily observed in an Orff music lesson. There is very much a sense of community in the interaction of the various members of the class in their dance, singing, and instrumental ensembles. The organization of music is continually focused upon through the manipulation of musical form with the *ostinato, bordun, coda,* and *introduction.* Orff teaching and the resulting class performances are very expressive. In fact, the expressive character of music is often the deciding factor in the lesson. (For example, instrument sounds may be used to enhance the images, elements, or characters in a song.) Musical independence is gained through the development of individual performance skill, especially improvisation, and self-esteem is a natural by-product of group and individual performance.

Choksy and her colleagues have identified "a basic continuum" for Orff music lessons. Each lesson moves from "imitation of the teacher" to "creation by the students." A sequence for an individual lesson follows.

1. an exercise or game which contains the kernel (a melodic or rhythmic pattern) of the element to be explored
2. conversation or communal play with the kernel by the students, until competency with it is demonstrated
3. play or ensemble work with the kernel within forms and in various media
4. creation of "The Piece" from the kernel
5. performance (this must be at a high level for even the simplest of experiences)

(Adapted from Choksy/Abramson/Gillespie/Woods, *Teaching Music in the Twentieth Century,* Copyright 1986, page 140. Reprinted by permission of Prentice Hall, Englewood Cliffs, NJ.)

The Orff process is very attractive to both students and teachers. Some school systems have even adapted system wide Orff music programs. This popularity is probably due to the performance aspects of the Orff process. One cannot be passive in an Orff music class. The various explorations and improvisations ultimately lead to musical works which are performed with a high degree of expressive quality. The following is an example of how an Orff specialist might create a "set piece" from a folk song.

Rain Come Wet Me

After learning the folk song through chant and speech activities. The teacher may have the class experiment with different words to create *ostinato* patterns to accompany *Rain Come Wet Me*. "Rain rain go away", "pitter patter," and "drip drop" may be related to a song about rain. The children would first chant the words as different accompanying *ostinato* parts. Next they would transfer the *ostinato* patterns to body percussion. For example, they would pat the rhythm of "rain rain go away" on their thighs. (Body percussion includes snapping, clapping, patting, and stamping.)

After the children have developed competency in patting the various ostinato parts on their thighs, they transfer the patting patterns to the barred instruments of the Orff instrumentarium. In the above example, SG, AX, and BX indicate soprano glockenspiel, alto xylophone, and bass xylophone respectively. These instruments may be prepared by removing all the pitch bars except the ones that the children will play. After the instruments have been prepared, the children may play (with mallets) the *ostinato* patterns on the respective instruments.

The teacher and class may further develop the above piece by creating an *introduction* and a *coda* . The complete "rain rain go away" chant may be used as an *introduction*. Perhaps the class may decide to improvise a "thunderstorm" as a *coda*. Large drums or timpani, cymbals, and the larger barred instruments may be utilized to create thunder and lightning. Slow *glissandos* (pulling the mallet across all the tone bars) on the smaller barred instruments may be the "sound of the sun" coming from behind the clouds. A wind chime may be the "sound of a rainbow."

As the piece develops it may be extended into a "rain rondo" with a recurring *Rain Come Wet Me* as the "A" section. The children may even perform a rain dance and dramatize different aspects of the piece. As the children experiment and explore the different aspects of *Rain Come Wet Me* they increase their sensitivity to form, rhythm, melody, and expression in music, and they increase their performance skills. It is readily observable why the Orff process is popular with so many teachers and students.

MUSIC TEXTBOOK SERIES

Music textbook series have been published and used in the public schools since the 19th century. Just as school systems adopt certain textbook series for math, language arts, and science, many school systems also adopt textbook series for music. There are a variety of music textbook series available today. Some popular series are *The World of Music* published by Silver Burdett and Ginn, *Music and You* published by Macmillan, and *The Music Book* published by Holt, Rinehart, and Winston. These texts are designed to be used by the classroom teacher or the music specialist. They have several common characteristics.

Each series is published with a teacher's edition, student books, and accompanying recordings for each grade level, K-6 or K-8. (Student textbooks are usually not published for kindergarten.) The teachers' editions contain an introduction and guide to the series which explains the philosophy behind the series, the goals and objectives of the series, and the organization of the textbook.

Goals and Objectives, and Organization

The philosophy of the different series may be very specific as to why music should be taught or it may refer to how music should be taught. One series is based upon a "generative approach" to music learning which "allows the learner to become more deeply involved in the aesthetic experience; aware of music as an avenue of human expression; and musically independent" (Boardman & Andress, 1984).

Another series lists its philosophy as: "participation by all students through singing, playing, moving, listening, creating, and writing; integration of traditional music practices with Orff, Kodaly, and Dalcroze; and sequenced concepts and skills help students to learn step-by-step through consistent introduction, review, creative activities, reinforcement and appraisal" (Staton, Staton, Davidson, & Snyder, 1988).

The goals and objectives of the different series (sometimes called scope and sequence) are very similar and generally follow research suggestions and common practices in the development of music concepts. For example, the kindergarten and first grade books emphasize the music concepts of loud and soft, fast and slow, different musical timbres, and high and low pitch. Textbooks for the older grade levels include more advanced concepts like harmony, singing in two parts, music reading, and performing on instruments like the guitar and recorder. Learning activities include singing, moving, creating, playing instruments, listening, and reading and writing music.

The organization of the different textbook series is also very similar. Lessons are grouped into units which may reflect learning activities like singing, moving, and playing, or seasons of the year. Each series has a core music curriculum or minimum plan of lessons supplemented by an extended plan. The teacher is advised to follow the core plan and to add extended lessons as needed, desired, or as time permits.

The individual lessons come with a detailed lesson plan and are supposedly organized sequentially. Each lesson plan may have objectives, materials listed, an introduction or motivation section (sometimes called getting started), the process or procedures of the lesson, and supplementary activities for exceptional children, extended learning, transfer, or integration into the nonmusic curriculum. These lessons are based upon the songs in the textbooks which are recorded and accompany each grade level. The lessons are easy to follow and designed for teachers who may or may not read or perform music. One series even has recorded music lessons by master teachers to be used as models for the user of the textbook.

Songs and Recordings

Perhaps the most attractive feature of the music textbook series is the recordings of the songs that make up the lessons. The recordings are high quality studio productions with professional musicians and orchestras. In most instances, the vocal parts are sung by adolescent and preadolescent children. The songs are a wide variety of traditional American folk songs, folk songs from other countries, songs for special days and seasons, specially composed songs, and classical music selections.

The songs and accompanying recordings may be used in a variety of ways. The recordings may be used as models for the children to imitate, especially those which use preadolescent singers. They may be used to initially learn a new song or, those that are recorded in stereo allow the vocal parts to be turned off so that the children in the classroom may sing with the recorded accompaniment. Some recordings are to accompany movement activities, others are for listening lessons, and some are to serve as examples of the music from other countries. The multicultural aspect of the recordings is very appropriate for today's education environment.

Listening Lessons and Guides

The professionally produced recordings which accompany the music textbook series are valuable tools for developing listening skills in the elementary music classroom. As mentioned in Chapter One, one of the outcomes of music education should be the ability to listen to music and describe how the elements of music are manipulated by the composer to create expression in music. In the elementary school the development of this skill begins with identifying the instruments of the orchestra, following tempo and dynamic changes in the music, identifying repetition and contrast, and following the contour of melodies. During the later years it may advance to identifying the form of a composition, compositional techniques, modulations and harmonic changes, and following the score of a symphony. The development of this listening skill is very important to the aesthetic experience and value of music to living. It is also an important part of "critical thinking" in music, a term very much in vogue in contemporary education.

There appears to be two general ways of presenting listening lessons in the textbook series. One example is provided by Silver Burdett and Ginn which utilizes "Call Charts" which ask the question "What do you hear?" Students are to circle whether the music is fast or slow or high or low, etc. (depending on the concept) as different selections are played. The recording features a recorded adult voice which identifies the selections by numbers. The following is an example of a listening chart from Silver Burdett and Ginn.

WHAT DO YOU HEAR? 2: Dynamics - recording 4

What do you hear? Some of the following pieces are soft. Others are loud. Each time a number is called, decide whether the music is soft or loud. If you think the music is soft, draw a circle around the word SOFT. If you think the music is loud, draw a circle around the word LOUD. Listen. Then circle what you hear. (recorded instructions)

1. SOFT LOUD (*Raise a Ruckus*)

2. SOFT LOUD (Lulla, *Lullaby*)

3. SOFT LOUD (Ravel, Maurice: *Bolero*)

4. SOFT LOUD (Ravel, Maurice: *Bolero*)

Here are the correct answers. Were you able to tell the difference between soft and loud? The more you can *hear* in music, the more you can *feel* in music. (recorded instructions) (*Silver Burdett Music, Centennial Edition, Teacher's Edition 1.* 1985, page 75, used with permission)

Another format for the listening lesson is the "listening map" or guide. This format utilizes a combination of pictures, drawn figures, and words to guide the student through the piece. Beginning on the next page is an example of a listening map to the first two minutes of Camille Saint-Saens' *Dance Macabre*. The scene is set in the grave yard as the clock (the harp) strikes twelve. The listener hears the footsteps of the devil as he approaches to tune his fiddle. After the devil tunes his fiddle the skeletons play their theme (melody) on flute and then the strings. Next a ghost plays his theme on the violin followed by the skeleton and then the devil. Each figure in the example depicts a theme and the primary instruments that perform.

The Kodaly approach to listening is different from the ones mentioned above. Kodaly practitioners believe that children should not listen to recorded music until the latter stages of their elementary schooling. Listening lessons for young children in the Kodaly method concentrate on listening to the teacher sing or to other members of the class. When recorded music is listened to, the teacher prepares (familiarizes the students) the selection by having the students learn to sing in "movable do" the principle themes of the selection. Then, when the recording is played, the children are already familiar with the major parts of the work. They are asked to identify how the composer may have manipulated the various themes of the work. For example, the teacher might ask. "How did Beethoven change the rhythm of the melody?"

All of the above approaches appear to be successful in the development of listening skill in elementary age school children. The Kodaly method may be more appropriate with older children (as it is designed for) whereas the use of pictures and graphics may be more effective with younger children. Research indicates both approaches are successful with actual music notation (following a score or melodic line) being effective with older children.

Two important aspects of developing listening skill in young children are the selection of music to be listened to and the focus of the listening activity. Music for listening activities should have "attention drawing" characteristics. That is, it should feature obvious contrasts in dynamics, tempo, rhythm, melody, and instruments. Young children will not attend to slow, soft music. Music educators do not begin listening activities with string quartets. They select music with obvious contrasts such as the *In the Hall of the Mountain King* from the *Peer Gynt Suite* by Grieg. This work, as explained in Chapter One, features one rhythm pattern and melody that is continually repeated with obvious changes in tempo, dynamics, and instrumental color (timbre).

Dance Macabre

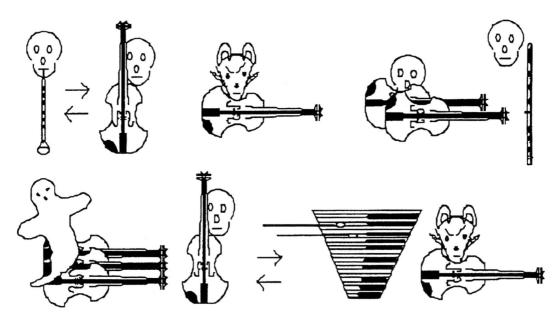

The other important aspect of listening is the focus of the activity. The students should listen for a specific element or to answer a specific question. Just as when students are attempting to learn a song, a motivation question or idea will greatly aid first attempts at focused listening. This may be as simple as "how many different instruments play the melody" or as sophisticated as "what is repeated and what changes." The students must have something to guide their listening. A specific question to answer or a map to follow will greatly increase the probability of success in listening activities.

One other important principle can also influence the listening activity. Teachers should not forget the importance of repetition and familiarity in learning music. The more familiar students are with a selection the more successful will they be in listening. Informal playings of selections to be listened to will increase the likelihood of successful focused listening activities. Playing a selection before or after a class or as a background to other activities will subconsciously prepare the students for later directed listening.

Music Textbook Series in the Classroom

The music textbook series are valuable source materials for the music specialist and the classroom teacher. For example, the indexes to the teacher's editions are divided into categories such as social studies, music concepts, holiday, seasonal, and special occasion songs, poems, programs and dramatizations, traditional folk songs, action songs and game songs, historical figures, health and safety, songs from other countries, and curriculum connections. These indexes make it very easy for the music specialist or classroom teacher to find a song or lesson to use for specific applications like a certain holiday, foreign country, or historical period. The accompanying recordings are an added plus. The more contemporary editions also have Kodaly and Orff guidelines so that the teachers who practice these methods may also use the textbook series.

A review of the lesson plans from two different series reveals the basic instructional strategies common to all music text books. A lesson on "high and low" from *Music and You Grade K* (Staton, Staton, Davidson, & Snyder,1988) utilizes a large chart with high and low pictures while a lesson on "high and low" from *Silver Burdett Centennial Edition Book 1* (Crook, Reimer, & Walker, 1985) utilizes a song about big and little pigs and the low (oink) and high (wee) sounds they make. The objectives to both lessons are similar. The *Music and You* lesson objective is "To hear, play, and identify high and low sounds." (p. 84) The *Silver Burdett* objectives include "Recognizing high and low notes in songs" and "high and low registers in listening selections." (p. xx) The following are excerpts from the lesson plans on "high and low" from each series.

Music and You Grade K

1. Introduce the concept of high and low pitch. Have the children: Look at Chart 22 (provided with the series) and identify the different positions of the two packages (one is low and one is high). Say *low* in a low voice or high in a *high* voice as you randomly point to the high or low package.

2. Introduce "Play Me a Song" to practice identifying low and high. Have the children: Listen to "Play Me a Song" (recorded). (Point to the low package on the low notes and the high package on the high notes.) Listen as you show them low D and high D on a Xylophone or other pitched barred instrument. Move to show low or high as you randomly play low D and high D. (Staton, Staton, Davidson, & Snyder, 1988. p. 84)

Silver Burdett Centennial Edition Book 1

1. As children listen to the recording (Three Little Pigs), encourage them to join in on the animal sounds.

2. Ask these questions: Which animal sounds were high? (Wee-wee-wee") Which sounds were low? (Oink, oink, oink)

3. When children know the song, call attention to the low-sounding instrument (bassoon) that plays during the low *oink, oink, oink's*, and the high-sounding instrument (piccolo) that echoes the high *wee-wee-wee's*. (Crook, Reimer, & Walker,1985, p. 76)

As can be seen the objectives and lesson plans are easy to understand, and with the recordings, they are easy to teach. In many instances a classroom teacher with very little musical skill can present an effective music lesson with the music textbook series.

Although the music textbook series are very attractive, they are not without fault. One weakness of the textbook series appears to be in their sequence and lack of depth. One analysis of a current series revealed that the sequence of musical learnings appeared to be fragmented and redundant. The analysis suggested that learning music in this series meant learning discrete elements of music, a folk song repertoire, and clapping a steady beat (May, Lantz, & Rohr, 1990).

Some of the lessons appear to be repetitive or below the level of many students and very few of the series attempt to develop music reading and singing skills. In most instances there is no discussion of proper singing technique. Children may not learn to sing by mimicking recordings. Some believe that singing with recordings may actually inhibit the development of singing skill. Students may not be able to hear themselves properly, and the sophisticated professional accompaniment may be distracting rather than helpful. The value of music lessons that do not lead to singing and music reading skill (even on an elementary level) must be questioned.

CHAPTER SUMMARY

Although there are many approaches to music education in the elementary school, Kodaly, Orff, and the music textbooks series are the most popular. The Kodaly method is a very systematic approach to music education. Its major emphasis is on singing and the sequential arrangement of the curriculum according to culture and child development characteristics. The Orff approach focuses on movement, chant, creativity, and instrumental play. Its popularity is probably due to its performance orientation. Music textbook series have been used since the 19th century. They are a valuable source material for music educators and classroom teachers.

Although there are authorities who believe in the use of one of the above methods over others, in reality, most elementary music programs utilize elements of each. The Kodaly method gives music specialists a very good means for organizing the content of elementary music. The systematic learning of melodic and rhythm patterns combined with the literacy and singing aspects of Kodaly are important aspects of many programs. These same programs will use the Orff instruments and creative activities, and incorporate songs and recordings from the textbook series for special needs, seasons, movement activities, and listening lessons. An informed observer will notice elements of Kodaly, Orff, and the textbook series in most American elementary music classes.

Suggested Activities

1. Observe elementary music classes and attempt to categorize the curriculum and activities according to Kodaly, Orff, and the textbook series.

2. If possible, interview music teachers who specialize in Kodaly or Orff. Have them describe the benefits and philosophy of each approach.

3. Develop some Orff "set pieces" from rhymes and chants. Use vocal ostinatos, transfer them to body percussion (stamp, pat, clap, snap), then to the Orff mallet instruments. Use pitches from the pentatonic scale to create a melody. For example "Georgy Porgy" might be developed into the following.

Georgy Porgy

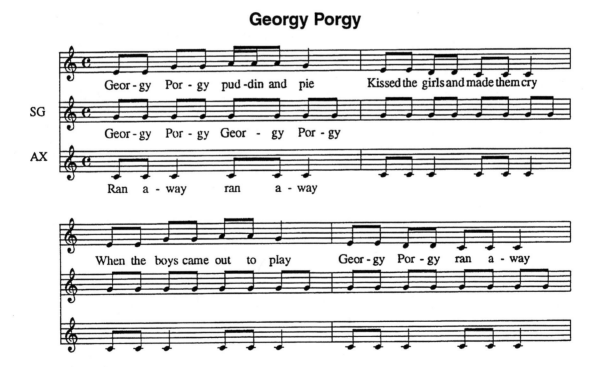

Some good examples of "set pieces" may be found in the following source materials:

Saliba, K. K. (1976). *Safari: A musical adventure.* Melville, N. Y.: Belwin Mills Publishing Corporation.

Frazee, J., & Steen, A. *This is the day: Songs for special days.* Melville, N. Y.: Schmitt, Hall & McCreary.

Frazee, J., & Steen, A. (1979). *A baker's dozen: Classroom ensembles for voices, recorders, and Orff instruments.* Melville, N. Y.: Belwin Mills Publishing Corporation.

4. Practice presenting a music lesson (with recordings) from a music textbook series.

5. Discuss with music teachers the development of singing without accompaniment versus using recordings for singing activities.

6. Develop a listening lesson for an elementary music class. Select a piece with attention drawing characteristics and develop a focus question. Can you create a listening guide or map for your selection? The following is a listening map for the beginning of the trumpet part to Aaron Copland's *Fanfare for the Common Man*.

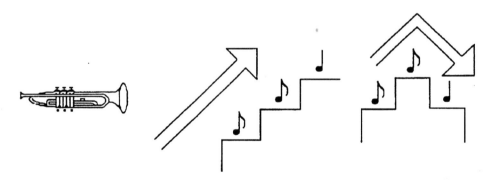

SUGGESTED RESOURCES

Choksy, L. (1981). *The Kodaly context: Creating an environment for musical learning.* Englewood Cliffs, N. J.: Prentice-Hall, Inc.

Frazee, J., & Kreuter, K. (1987). *Discovering Orff: A curriculum for music teachers.* New York: Schott.

Choksy, L., Abramson, R. M.; Gillespie, A. E., & Woods, D. (1986). *Teaching music in the twentieth century.* Englewood Cliffs, N. J.: Prentice-Hall, Inc.

May, W., Lantz, T., & Rohr, S. (1990). *Whose content, context and culture in elementary art and music textbooks?* East Lansing, MI: The Center for the Learning and Teaching of Elementary Subjects.

Music Textbook Series

Beethoven, J., Davidson, J., & Nadon-Gabrion, C. (1991). *World of music*. Morristown, NJ: Silver Burdett and Ginn.

Boardman, E., & Andress, B. (1984). *The music book*. New York: Holt, Rinehart, and Winston, Publishers.

Crook, E. Reimer, B., & Walker, D. (1985). *Silver Burdett Music: Centennial edition*. Morristown, NJ: Silver Burdett Company.

Staton, B., Staton, M., Davidson, M., & Snyder, S. (1988). *Music and you*. New York: Macmillan Publishing Company.

Chapter 5

MUSIC TO ENHANCE THE LEARNING ENVIRONMENT

Research indicates that very few classroom teachers teach music in their classrooms. The most common reason given for this phenomenon is that classroom teachers do not feel prepared to teach music. This is easily understood when one considers that classroom teachers usually have just one music methods class (two at the most) in undergraduate school. Without a fairly extensive musical background, it is unlikely that future classroom teachers will learn the skills, content, and methods necessary to teach music.

It would seem that what the future classroom teacher needs is an understanding of how music can be a positive force for learning throughout the classroom teacher's day. Then perhaps the classroom teacher will be motivated to use music to enhance the learning environment. Rather than teach music, the classroom teacher can use music as a powerful tool for learning.

THE POWER OF MUSIC

Research indicates that classroom teachers who use music and the other arts throughout the day will reap many positive rewards. During the early 70s a federally sponsored project called IMPACT (Interdisciplinary Model Programs in the Arts for Children and Teachers) developed elementary school programs which utilized the arts throughout the curriculum. At certain schools, art teams were brought in to work with teachers to integrate music, art, dance, and drama into the curriculum. Virtually every subject area included some component of the arts. One of IMPACT's goals was:

To develop ways of integrating the arts into all aspects of the school curriculum as a means of enhancing and improving the quality and quantity of aesthetic education offered in the school, and as a principal means for expanding the base for affective learning experiences in the total school curriculum (Mark, 1986, p. 92).

At the completion of the program, test results indicated that students who participated in the program were significantly above grade level in reading and other skills several years after their arts experiences. The test results also showed that students developed self-esteem through their arts experiences and their attitudes toward school improved. (Mark, 1986, page 92). In general, it appears that quality music and arts programs improve academic performance and attitudes toward school. In a summary of the research in this area Wolf (1977) found that:

> There may be measurable effects of music education on the development of cognitive skills and understanding. This seems to be true for both general transfer, i.e., 'learning how to learn,' and specific transfer. Specific transfer is particularly apparent in its effect on performance in the language arts. (Wolf, 1977, p. 19)

Hanshumaker (1986) looked at the research on the outcomes of music and arts education and concluded:

> 1. Arts instruction has a significant positive effect on basic language development and reading readiness.

> 2. Although links between music instruction and math achievement have been difficult to establish, it appears that daily music instruction has a significant, positive effect on math scores.

> 3. Arts activities foster positive attitudes toward school and the general curriculum. Schools in which the arts are an integral part of the curriculum experience lower rates of absenteeism when compared to schools where arts instruction is minimal and haphazard.

> 4. School time spent on music and other arts activities has no negative effect on academic achievement as reflected in either scores on standardized tests or general grade point average. (Hanshumaker, 1986, p. 10)

These positive effects of music are not new or surprising. Philosophers since the time of Plato and Aristotle have identified the "power of music" to affect human behavior. Music has always been a very important part of ceremony and symbolic meaning. Think of the effect of music in religion, athletics, politics, and advertising. Music is even used to control behavior in the work place, shopping malls, and super markets. If music can be so powerful in society, it also can be powerful in the school. Teachers can use this power to enhance the total learning environment.

Perhaps the most powerful use of music for the classroom teacher is in the development of positive attitudes toward school. School must be attractive if students are to attend and be motivated to learn. A school day where music is used to enhance the overall environment will be a rewarding day for the young student. Music and the arts enhance living; they can also enhance schooling.

Given the above, it would seem that music would be a very important part of every classroom teacher's pedagogy. Yet, as mentioned above, this is not true. Classroom teachers feel inadequately prepared to teach music. However, one does not need to teach music to reap the benefits of music in the classroom. One only needs to use music. The distinction is small but significant. The skills needed to utilize music throughout the day are considerably less than those needed to teach music. One only needs to be able to sing with reasonably good intonation, play recordings, and be able to organize movement activities and singing games.

MUSIC THROUGHOUT THE DAY

It would be very hard to integrate music into every class one teaches. However, there are numerous opportunities to use music throughout the day which do not require extra planning and extensive practice. If classroom teachers can sing or chant, and have access to some music textbook series, they can accomplish much for themselves and their students.

Classroom teachers should consider beginning the day with music. Today most classrooms have stereo systems. If not, quality stereo systems are relatively inexpensive to purchase. As the children enter the classroom in the morning the classroom teacher can play recordings of music. The teacher may have some recordings of Mozart, Haydn, or Beethoven (preferably something not too slow) playing informally. The teacher may list the title of the composition on the chalk board as in "This week we are listening to Mozart's *Eine Kleine Nachtmusik*." The teacher may also list other factors about the composition such as the dates of the composer's life and relate them to American history, or correlate the style of the music with art from the same period, or perhaps relate the music to a geographical area or culture. The teacher might write the following about *Eine Kleine Nachtmusik* on the chalk board.

This week we are listening to Mozart's Eine Kleine Nachtmusik. Mozart (1756-91) lived and composed music in Germany and Austria during the colonial and revolutionary war period. He was a child prodigy who composed his first music at age four. Eine Kleine Nachtmusik means "A little night music." It is one of a group of compositions that are sometimes called serenades. They were composed for garden parties, weddings, birthdays, or home concerts for Mozart's friends. Eine Kleine Nachtmusik was completed on August 10, 1787.

Just playing the music informally will enhance the atmosphere of the classroom. Children will look forward to entering the classroom. As the teacher repeats the playing throughout the week, the children will become more familiar with the music, their perception will be enhanced, and perhaps their preference for music will be influenced.

After the children have entered the classroom and it is time for the school day to begin, the teacher may sing a greeting song. This should be a song that can be rearranged to suit any particular needs like calling the roll or identifying students. The following are some greeting songs with suggestions on how they may be modified for particular purposes. The teacher may also create special greeting songs from pentatonic and descending scale patterns.

Hello Everybody

Hello Everybody may be modified by using different colors for clothing, different body movements (e. g. pat pat pat your leg), or the beginning may be changed to "Goodbye everybody, have a nice day."

How Do You Do

The teacher may keep adding the student's names till everyone's name has been sung or point to different students. Everyone sings the names. The beginning could be changed to "Now it's time to go—, to go, etc.

Hello

Greetings

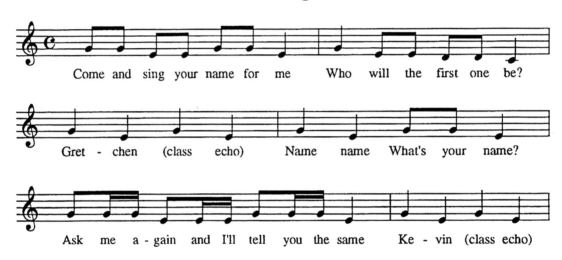

("Come and Sing Your Name for Me" is from *Music Book O*, Copyright 1976 MMB Music, Inc., Saint Louis. Reprinted with permission.)

Descending Scale Greeting

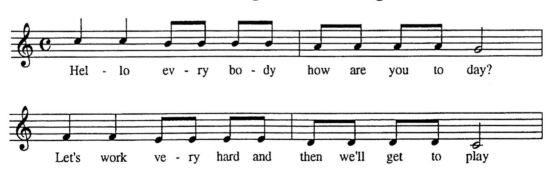

A good principle to remember is that it is very important to begin the day and individual lessons with an activity that everyone can participate in successfully. If everyone begins the day feeling successful and positive they are likely to be positive about the activities and events that follow. When they think of their school activities, children will remember how the day began. Positive feelings developed through music will enhance their reflections about school.

Other opportunities to use music throughout the day are for changing activities or for routine activities such as going outside, going to lunch, or for story time. The teacher may create original songs from pentatonic patterns or change the words to familiar tunes to create music for these activities. The following are some examples of routine activities songs. Familiar songs like *London Bridge, Are You Sleeping*, and *The Muffin Man* are easily modified for routine purposes.

Going to Lunch

Now the Day is Done

(mi sol la)

Story Time

(*Hot Cross Buns*)

Sto - ry time   Sto - ry time   Let's form a cir-cle now it's sto - ry time

Going Outside

(*do la sol*)

How are you   I   am fine   Let's get to-ge-ther and   go out-side

Early childhood teachers will find that playing recordings for quiet time will enhance this part of the day for their children. Here the tempo should be slower with a steady sustained pulse. Music therapists frequently use the sedative and soothing aspect of music. It also can be used as a calming influence with young children. Classics like Bach's *Air on a G String* or Pachelbel's *Canon* work well for quiet time. One researcher has found that music can have a significant calming effect on children when used immediately after play time (Giles,1991).

Children often enjoy singing or listening to music while doing individual work. They may sing along with recordings while writing in their daily journals or during visual art activities. When music is part of the normal routine children may even request to sing while they work. Recordings by Raffi, Hap Palmer, and Greg and Steve contain many songs appropriate for singing or listening during individual work periods.

Just as the beginning of the day is important, so is the end of the day. The last thing children should remember about school should be an activity that left them feeling successful and emotionally content. Again, music is perfectly suited for developing these feelings. A quiet listening time, song, or rhythmic chant as the children pack away should stimulate positive feelings about school and the preceding day. The teacher may create original songs from pentatonic patterns, change the words to familiar songs, sing familiar songs, or play appropriate recordings.

A word of caution should be expressed about playing recordings for children at school. Popular music, particularly of the Top 40 style, should not be played on a regular basis for elementary age children. Children are already familiar with this music. They learn very little from listening to popular music. On occasion a popular music selection may be used as a reward for behavior or achievement, but school should be a place where students are exposed to things they normally will not experience outside of school. If children do not hear classical, folk, and jazz music in school, they may not hear it at all. There is a wealth of classical, folk, and jazz music that is unfamiliar to school children. Developing familiarity with this music will enhance their perceptual skills, increase their cultural awareness, and make their lives more meaningful.

SINGING GAMES AND MOVEMENT ACTIVITIES

One of the most important aspects of music with young children is movement. The importance of movement activities for elementary students should not be underestimated. Children need to move. Movement stimulates brain activity, muscle development, and strengthens bone structure. Some research even indicates that when movement is restricted, intellectual development is stunted. The psychomotor domain is a major part of learning and child development.

The music specialist teaches movement to students as part of their regularly scheduled music classes. Unfortunately, at the most, students will have music only twice a week. Then, the music specialist may have so many skills to teach that movement may be offered only once a week and sometimes not at all.

Movement is one aspect of music teaching and learning where the classroom teacher can contribute significantly. Young children naturally sing and move when they play and they have many singing games that may be used to foster their movement development. Young girls, in particular, often play singing games that are basically chants accompanied by hand claps and movements (often called hand jive).

Singing games and movement activities are naturally suited for the playground or gym. They are an enjoyable means for encouraging group activity and cooperation. They help develop psychomotor coordination, pulse sensitivity and rhythm skill, self confidence, the ability to follow directions, and they are just plain fun.

Managing Movement Activities

There are some management problems that should be considered before attempting to lead movement activities with young children. First, space is an essential requirement. The children should have enough space to move freely without fear of colliding with one another or desks, chairs, and other objects. A teacher must establish a few basic rules before beginning the singing game. These may be simply "do not touch one another" or "no pushing, shoving, or silly behavior." The rules should also include a signal for stopping the game. A signal such as a hand clap, whistle, or even a code word like "freeze" often works better than just asking the children to stop. The children should be aware of the rules before the movement activity begins.

A problem often occurs with singing games when children are asked to form a circle or to form two lines. Young children have difficulty forming circles and lines. This problem may be solved by drawing a circle or two lines on the ground or floor and asking the children to take places on the lines. The teacher might also have the children form a single line and then lead the line into a circle or break the line to form two confronting lines. This may sound simplistic, but many movement games call for formations that the children cannot form without practice.

A final consideration should be how the game is taught. It is much easier to model a movement activity for children than it is to explain the movements. When a teacher models for children one must be careful that the children do not become confused about right and left motions. Sometimes "mirroring" by the teacher may solve this potential problem. Another effective means for learning the movements to an activity is to practice the movements individually (as in a single line) as the children are learning the accompanying song. For example, the movements to John Kanaka may be practiced individually before they are done in a double line or circle.

John Kanaka

Directions to John Kanaka

Formation - two circles facing (inner and outer) or two lines facing

1 - Circles or lines go around partner to left and step backwards to start-ing position (do si do). On John (stamp foot), on Ka na ka na ka (pat thighs to rhythm of words), on too la (clap hands), and on ay (clap partner's hands)

2 - Same as 1

3 - Change partners by inner circle moving four steps to right on too la ay - too la ay, then repeat stamp pat clap movements to John Kanaka naka.

Movement and Basic Skills

Movement can also be an attractive means for teaching what are often called basic skills. Young children need to learn their left and right, numbers, the alphabet, basic spatial relationships, colors, shapes, health and safety, and develop coordination. Movement activities are natural means for helping young children learn these basic skills. The Hap Palmer *Learning Basic Skills Through Music* recordings contain many activities for learning basic skills. *Marching Around the Alphabet* and *The Number March* are but two examples of learning basic skills through music and movement. The *We All Live Together* series by Greg and Steve also has basic skills movement activities. *The ABC Rock, Shapes,* and *Days of the Week* are included in these volumes.

The classroom teacher may also create movement activities to accompany the learning of basic skills. A basic "pat", or for older children, a "pat clap" for the pulse, can make learning the alphabet or other basic memorizations fun.

CREATING SPECIAL SONGS AND CHANTS

The classroom teacher may want to create some original songs or chants for use throughout the day, or to aid in the teaching of basic skills. The easiest way to accomplish this is to change the words to a familiar song. *Are You Sleeping* or *Mary Had a Little Lamb* lend themselves easily to this sort of modification. A good source for songs and useful modifications is *Piggy Back Songs* compiled by Jean Warren (1983).

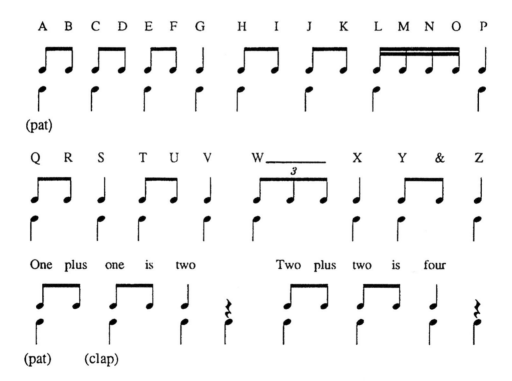

Rain Drops

(Twinkle Twinkle Little Star)

Rain drops rain drops all around,
Splish and splash and on the ground.
See them here and see them there,
Rain drops rain drops ev-ry where.
Rain drops rain drops all around,
Splish and splash and on the ground.

When creating original songs and chants the teacher should remember the basic principle of form in music. That is, the song must have repetition. Simple binary form works very well. This could be as simple as two contrasting phrases repeated or two contrasting sections. It is recommended that the beginning composer use melodic patterns from the pentatonic scale. These should be easy to sing and in the proper range. Descending patterns work well. Develop form by repetition and end on either *do* or *la*. The following example illustrates the composition of an original song from the pentatonic scale.

An Original Pentatonic Song

Question (with repetition)

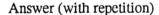

Answer (with repetition)

Another good vehicle for special songs is the descending major scale (high *do* to low *do*). The following are examples of special songs on the descending major scale.

Autumn Leaves or Falling

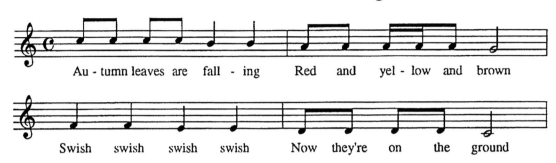

Spring

For those teachers who feel uncomfortable singing, rhythmic chant will work just as well as melodic songs. Rhythm patterns such as *ta ta ti ti ta, ti ti ta ti ti ta*, and *ti ti ti ti ta ta* work well with most words. Or, the teacher may wish to use the rhythm patterns of familiar songs. In either case the natural rhythm of the words should be the determining factor. In some instances a natural word rhythm may be changed to fit a certain meter; however, this may make the chant awkward. Simple duple meter or compound meter are the most common meters for chant. Teachers should emphasize the pulse in their chant and experiment with adding finger snaps and other body percussion sounds for rests. The following example illustrates original chant for the classroom.

Original Chant

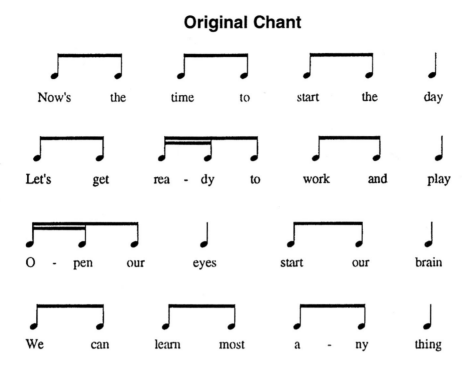

Now's   the   time   to   start   the   day

Let's   get   rea - dy   to   work   and   play

O - pen   our   eyes   start   our   brain

We   can   learn   most   a - ny   thing

INTEGRATING MUSIC INTO THE CURRICULUM

A common element in many of today's elementary and middle schools is the organization of curriculum around topics and concepts. Rather than separating learning into distinct disciplines, many schools attempt to coordinate or integrate learning throughout the curriculum through the use of organizational topics or concepts. This integrated curriculum or interdisciplinary learning is an attempt to make learning more meaningful for students. After all, the real world is not separated into distinct disciplines. One's skills in the disciplines (math, language, science) interact and integrate throughout one's existence. We don't experience science for a little while and then need math and language. Our existence draws upon an integrated knowledge of all the disciplines, even the arts.

The use of topical and conceptual themes leads students to discover how math, science, social studies, and language arts are applied to answer questions pertaining to their everyday existence. For example, students studying transportation or highways in their community will need to apply all of the above mentioned disciplines as they discover how their transportation system evolved over time, what future transportation needs might be, and how these needs may be met.

Some common topics and concepts that are used as organizers for learning are the following:

Topical themes	Concept themes
Our town	Change
Going to school	Diversity
Recycling	Patterns
Oceans	Texture
Rain forests	Expression
Travel	Conflict
Living things	Independence

Topical themes appear to be more appropriate for younger grades while some conceptual organizers may be more appropriate for the older grades. Of course topical and conceptual themes may overlap. For instance, texture would be a good concept theme to include in a learning unit on rain forests. The different levels of the rain forest make a very complex texture of life. Another example of overlap might be "Our town" and "change." As children study their town they become aware of the changes that have occurred, why they have occurred, and what changes may occur in the future. Change and the causes and effects of change may be illustrated through all the disciplines of learning in the school.

Themes for organizing learning should be based upon real life existence and the concepts that permeate existence. The important criterion is that the topic or theme must be capable of leading to exploration and learning throughout the traditional disciplines of knowledge. Just imagine where the study of something as simple as the wheel could lead to in history, math, geometry, art and language. Students could attempt to determine when wheels first appeared in history, the mathematical and geometrical properties of circles, the physics of size and weight and distance, circle games, form in music that is circular, circles and wheels in nature and art, etc.

There are two basic ways the classroom teacher might utilize music in an interdisciplinary curriculum. One is through association or connection. The classroom teacher uses music to support learning about the theme or topic. For example, the classroom teacher may teach the children songs about insects when studying insects or "Ten Little Indians" as a counting exercise in math. There is nothing wrong with using music to support other subjects in this manner but music can also be used to illustrate a concept in another subject. Many would call this latter method true integration. For example, there are patterns in music, math, poetry, and social studies. Each discipline may illustrate the concept of pattern within its own structure.

Patterns in Music

Melodic patterns
Rhythm patterns
Repeated patterns
Form in music

Patterns in Science

Structures of molecules
Patterns of behavior
Life cycles
The solar system

Patterns in Social Studies

Patterns of social development
Patterns of immigration
Patterns in economics
Patterns in industry

Patterns in Mathematics

Number patterns
Geometric patterns
Patterns in graphs

Another example of true integration might occur in a unit on "Our Town." As the students discover how their town has changed during different historical periods and with the influx of different cultures, music from the different time periods and cultures can be used to illustrate characteristics of that period or culture. Or students might create an original song that is reflective of the character of their town. Is the town a busy, compact, bustling place, or a quiet sleepy village? Existing music might also be used to illustrate the environment of their town. *An American in Paris* by George Gershwin sounds very much like a busy city.

When exploring the use of music in an interdisciplinary unit one should try to utilize music as a connection and true integration. The use of topics and concepts together will facilitate the inclusion of music at both levels.

Class Activity

Follow these guidelines to develop your own interdisciplinary units and lessons. First identify your topic and accompanying concepts. This may be the most difficult part of the whole process. Selecting appropriate topics and concepts to organize learning throughout the different disciplines in school requires a lot of thought. Some places to look for themes are the following: Things (buildings, machines); Food; Events; Places; People; Ideas/Concepts; Endeavors; Phenomena; Issues; and Sports.

Once a topic or theme has been selected, describe the study and its outcomes. What will the students do, discover and conclude from their study? Be general enough in your description to allow for all the different branches of study that may occur. After the study is described, list the disciplines to be included in the study and their accompanying topics, concepts, and learning activities.

Use the following unit as a guide to develop an interdisciplinary model that includes music.

The Rain Forest
(an example of an interdisciplinary unit for 2nd or 3rd grade)

1. Topic & concepts

The rain forest—texture

2. Describe the Study and Its Outcomes

The students will study the existence of the rain forests, the environment that supports them, and the different life forms and accompanying ecology of the rain forests. The students will identify the different animals and types of plants in rain forests, the ecological and environmental conditions necessary for rain forests to exist, and the products harvested from the rain forests. They will investigate the effect of the rain forests on the environment and draw conclusions about the survival of the rain forests.

3. Interdisciplinary Studies

Science—Life forms (plant and animal), environment, food sources, and physiology of the different levels (texture) of canopy, climates.

Language Arts—Poetry, stories about rain forest peoples, creating original poetry about the rain forest.

Social Studies—Where are the rain forests, geographical differences, the cultures of the rain forest and their history.

Music—Music from the rain forest cultures, music with complex textures, creating original musical textures with poetry and Orff instruments, rhythms of bird, plant, and animal names, percussion instruments.

Math—Measuring the effects of acid rain, logging, and other industry, comparing sizes and heights of different canopy levels and the trees in them, patterns of growth and population, graphic representation of the decline in the rain forests.

Music and Rain Forests

Texture—The sounds of the rain forest can form a changing and complex texture much like the different levels of ecology in the rain forest. A rain forest has three different layers of life, the canopy, the understory, and the forest floor. These levels can be further divided into emergents (the very top trees), middle layer (canopy), and the shrub and herb layers (understory). The different animals and plants throughout these layers make a very complex texture. Have the class explore vocal, body percussion, and classroom instrument sounds to create a tonal texture similar to the rain forest. The rhythms of birds, plants, and animal names may be performed on Orff instruments to illustrate the different life forms at each level. Combining them all will create a texture much like the rain forest.

Texture may also be illustrated through existing music. Have the class listen to different works with different textures. Which would be more representative of the texture of a rain forest? Why? Listen to parts of Debussy's *Afternoon of a Faun*, Stravinsky's *Rite of Spring*, and the *Aviary* from *Carnival of the Animals* by Saint Saens.

Music of rain forest cultures—(South and Central America, Indonesia, Africa) The Mayan civilization developed in what were the great rain forests of Central America. The Mayan musical instruments were gourds filled with seeds or pebbles, drums made out of logs, and trumpet-like wooden instruments. Search music textbook series for music from South and Central America. Create classroom gourd and log drum instruments and perhaps a bamboo flute. Play a recording of Indonesian Gamelan music. Research the type of musical instruments found in Indonesia.

Discuss the role of music in African cultures. Play recordings and sing songs from the textbook series. Compare and contrast the musics of each culture.

Create original poetry about the birds and animals that live in the forest. Utilize the rhythm of their names to create expressive sounds to accompany the poetry.

Stories about the Rain forest—*The Great Kapok Tree* by Lynne Cherry

This story is about a man who comes into the rain forest to cut down a kapok tree. He begins chopping but soon grows tired and takes a nap. While he is asleep, the various animals from the rain forest come down from the tree and whisper into his ear. They describe the value of the kapok tree in their lives and plead for the man not to cut it down. He awakens surrounded by all of the animals and decides not to cut down the tree.

Develop a theme, and specific motifs for each animal with Orff and classroom instruments.

walking in the forest
the sound of chopping, chop! whack!
boa constrictor
a bee
a troupe of monkeys
toucan
macaw and cock of the rock
small tree frog
jaguar
four tree porcupines
anteaters
three-toed sloth
a child from the Yanomano tribe
strange and beautiful flowers
fragrant perfume of the flowers
steamy mist rising from the forest floor.

Cherry, Lynne. (1990). *The great kapok tree. A tale of the Amazon rain forest.* NY: Gulliver Books, Harcourt Brace Jovanovich, Publishers.

Animals of the Rain Forest
(texture piece)

toucans
parrots
hoatzin (stink bird)
dodo birds (extinct)
red legged honey creeper
blue morhpho butterfly

walking stick
parsol ants
azteca ants

silky anteater
three toed sloth
maues marmoset - monkey
howling monkey

boa constrictor
coral snake
poison arrow frog
golden toad
jaguar
ocelot

PROCESS—Select instrument sounds from high to low to represent the different animals. Perform the rhythm of the animal names by groups to create a rain forest texture. All the birds could be one instrument, the butterflies another, and the insects another, etc. Repeat the patterns until the whole forest is included.

Rain Forest Texture

High Instruments

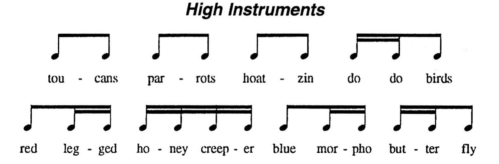

Middle Instruments

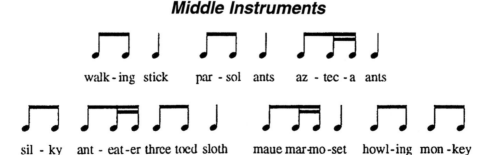

Low Instruments

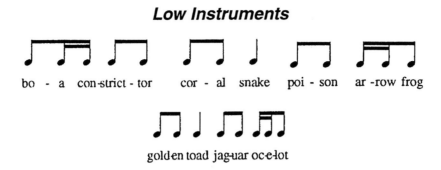

bo - a con-strict - tor   cor - al snake   poi - son   ar -row frog

golden toad jag-uar oc-e-lot

For those classroom teachers not teaching interdisciplinary units organized by topics and concepts, music may still be integrated with particular subject areas, both as a connection or to illustrate concepts common to both the subject area and music.

Language Arts, Geography and History (or Social Studies) seem the most appropriate for music integration although there are some relationships between music and science. One teacher has reported success with using Bach and Mozart to accompany group mathematics activities or while students worked practice problems. This teacher also used the *William Tell Overture* during chalk board games and contests (Stewart, 1991).

Music can enhance some subject matters whereas in others it may just represent a way of making the subject matter entertaining. In the latter instance, music might actually distract from the subject. There are valid ways to integrate music into the curriculum. They should not distract from the subject at hand or be an extra burden to the classroom teacher.

Music and Language Arts

Music and Language Arts go together naturally. Music has a direct relationship to language arts in that research indicates that music enhances certain language arts skills. Singing songs can naturally enhance vocabulary and listening lessons can develop the ability to focus and sequence events. One of the most natural links between music and language arts is through poetry. The ancient philosophers believed that music was tonal poetry and that music should enhance the words and meaning of poetry.

The classroom teacher may use rhythmic chant and singing to develop basic language skills. Or, language arts experiences may be enhanced by the use of musical effects to dramatize characters and emotions in stories and poetry. Many Orff practitioners have developed ideas for the dramatization of speech and poetry. For example, the Orff instruments or other classroom instruments, and in some cases, the synthesizer, may be used to enhance the emotional effect of character description and plot in a story or poem. These musical accompaniments may be as simple as special sound effects for childhood limericks or as complex as a composed tone poem that actually tells a story. In the first instance consider the following version of Humpty Dumpty.

> Humpty Dumpty sat on a wall (class sighs in a relaxed way)
> Humpty Dumpty had a great fall (voice falls ahhhhhh)
> All the king's horses (tongue clicking sounds)
> And all the king's men (clear throats with authority)
> Couldn't put Humpty together again (sad ooooooo)*

(Adapted from Frazee, *Discovering Orff* copyright Schott Music Corporation, 1987, All rights reserved. Used by permission of European American Music Distributors Corporation, sole U.S. and Canadian agent for Schott Music Corporation)

The above certainly enhances the emotional effect of Humpty Dumpty. It helps develop imagery which is a key element in language arts. The teacher may next wish to substitute instrumental sounds for class vocalizations.

> Humpty Dumpty sat on a wall (slow descending gliss on xylophone)
> Humpty Dumpty had a great fall (drum crash or fast gliss on xylophone)
> All the king's horses (wood blocks)
> And all the king's men (hand drum roll or tremolo)
> Couldn't put Humpty together again (tremolo on low xylophones)

The following example illustrates how the Orff process may enhance the language arts experience.

The Wind

from *A Child's Garden of Verses* by Robert Louis Stevenson

Theme (play two times)

> I saw you toss the *kites* on high
> And blow the *birds* about the sky;
> And all around I heard you *pass*,
> Like ladies' *skirts* across the grass -
>   Oh wind, a-blowing all day long, (theme)
>   Oh wind, that sings so loud a song!

I saw the *different* things you did,
But always you *yourself* you hid.
I felt you push, I heard you *call*,
I could not see *yourself* at all -
    O wind, a-blowing all day long, (theme)
    O wind that sings so loud a song!

Coda—Play the sounds for each word in sequence

PROCESS—Develop an introduction and theme by playing the rhythm of the repeating couplet on mallet instruments set in pentatonic.

Theme (play rhythm two times)

Oh   wind   a   blow - ing   all   day long

Write the underlined words on the chalk board and have the students choose sounds for each word.

kites—wind chimes, triangles, finger cymbals
birds—*glissandos* up and down on the mallet instruments
pass—slide hand back and forth over hand drums
skirts—maracas
different—play all instruments in sequence from the lowest to highest;
    for example—timpani, bass xylophones, alto metallophones, hand
    drums, wood blocks, maracas, glockenspiels, triangles, finger
    cymbals, wind chimes
yourself—*tremolo* on low mallet instruments
call—recorder
yourself—*tremolo* on low mallet instruments

PERFORM—Choose a narrator, perform the theme, play each word's sounds when spoken (play theme with repeating couplet at end of each verse), play *coda* (the sequence of word sounds).

As mentioned earlier, these musical effects or accompaniments can become quite sophisticated. An older class may create a tone poem to illustrate the plot of a story. The synthesizer and elements of the pentatonic scale can be used to create songs that represent each character and significant events in the story. Another class may create a radio show and use the Orff instruments for the sound effects to accompany the radio program.

Music is a very good means for stimulating the imagination for creative writing projects. A teacher may select a particularly descriptive composition such as *The Moldau* by Smetana or *Pictures at an Exhibition* by Mussorgsky and have the children listen and write a story to accompany the music. The children may wish to describe the events in the music as in "the violins play the rising melody" or they may imagine a story to accompany the musical events in the composition. Tone poems written during the 19th century and early 20th century by Franz Liszt, Bedrich Smetana, Camille Saint-Saens, and Richard Strauss are attempts to characterize stories in sound. Many of these compositions are appropriate for elementary age children. Some children may wish to draw stories, scenes, or even the music itself while others write a narrative. For example, Camille Saint-Saens' *Dance Macabre* (a tone poem) might be integrated with language arts, visual arts, and Halloween. This tone poem, sometimes called a symphonic poem, tells the following story.

Dance Macabre

Clock strikes midnight
Spirits awaken and dance
Rooster crows at dawn
Spirits go back to sleep

Second grade students could listen for elements of the story in the music while they draw and color a Halloween scene. The students then might write their own Halloween poems and discuss how music might "tell their story." Drawing and writing supposedly use different aspects of cognition (right brain versus left brain) and the inclusion of both activities is recommended to suit the different learning styles of children.

Whole Language

"Whole language" utilizes the whole of the language world. Students not only read, they listen, and they write. Language is treated as a whole rather than as separate units of speaking, listening, reading, and writing. The development of thought processes, communication, and interpretation is emphasized over learning specific words and spellings. Students read trade books and novels rather than basal series readers. Active learning, cooperative activities, and integrated units of instruction are important elements of "whole language." The following are examples of how a second grade teacher might use music activities in a "whole language approach" to language arts.

First the teacher plays a recording of a "new age" music selection for her class. The selection is performed with synthesizers and features many contrasts in timbre, dynamics, and special effects. The teacher instructs the class. "While you are listening write down what the music makes you think of. It can be anything, raindrops, wind, or whatever. You do not have to make sentences, you can write word lists or even a poem. After you have listened, we will read what you have written and then we will draw a collage of your impressions."

The children are motivated to do the activity as they listen and write. As the music plays, the teacher interjects at appropriate places, "What does this sound like? What does this make you think of?" After they have listened to the selection for a few minutes the teacher asks certain children to read what they have written. The children respond with the following.

A pond on a winter day

A rose blooming

Soft things

It makes me think I'm on the sea floating

It makes me think of all the things I did when I was 6 and 7 years old

Next, the teacher asks the children to draw as they listen to the selection again. Again, the children are highly motivated and after a few more minutes of listening they enthusiastically raise their hands to show their drawings to the class. Some drawings are descriptive and feature scenes that illustrate; others are more abstract.

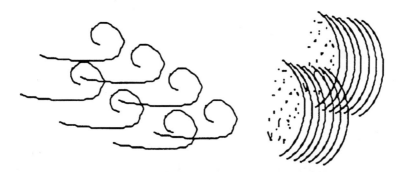

Over subsequent lessons, the teacher leads the children to create poems or "word paintings" that illustrate their thoughts while listening to the "new age" piece. These literary works are combined with the children's art illustrations to present a colorful collage for public display.

Listening to folk music can also be a valuable "whole language" experience for students. Again, a second grade teacher tells her class, "Today we are going to listen to some music that is just for a good time, for enjoyment. It is called old time, traditional, or bluegrass. The musician you are going to hear is Doc Watson. He lives in North Carolina in the mountains." The teacher plays the recording, *Doc Watson sings for Little Pickers*. The first selection is *Talking Guitar*. After listening for a few moments the teacher asks her students to name the words used for animals. The students respond with "tomcat, chicken, rooster, and muskrat." The teacher asks which are compound words and helps the children define "muskrat." She then leads a discussion about animals on farms and how farm life is very different from what most experience today.

The next selection on the recording is *Mole in the Ground*. The teacher asks the students "to listen for what we wish." The song includes "I wish I were a lizard in the spring, mole in the ground," and other wishes. After listening, the teacher asks the children to "tell us about a time that you made a wish."

The class listens to one more folk song from the recording, *Frog went a Courtin* and lists words they hear that rhyme. During the class discussions of the words of the folk songs, the teacher has listed on the chalk board the words discussed and defined.

tomcat
chicken
rooster
muskrat mountain
mole

lizard
harmonica
June bug
cake
bake
snake

These words and others will be used by the children to write a story about life on a farm in the mountains. To close the activity, the teacher reads the children a short story, *The Relatives Came* (Rylant, 1985), about people visiting a farm and playing musical instruments.

Another "whole language" activity with music is composing new lyrics to familiar songs. A class may choose a familiar song such as *Rocky Mountain* or *Yankee Doodle* and create new lyrics to illustrate a story, idea, message, or emotion. The children should first study the lyrics of the familiar song for patterns, rhymes, and repetition. Then they may develop their own lyrics to fit the design of the familiar song. As the students develop the lyrics they consider rhyming words, meter, and the meaning and emotional effect of the words. As they work the students may change more and more of the familiar song until it evolves into an original song. For example, after they have created new lyrics, they may wish to change the contour of the melody or an important rhythm, or they may wish to add new ideas between the repeating verses as in a *rondo* form. The following example illustrates how the pattern "Rocky Mountain" might evolve in a song about pollution.

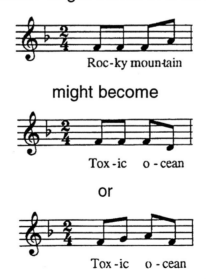

It is easy to see why music is such a valuable tool in language arts. It not only motivates but stimulates imagination and creativity. The following are recommendations for music and language that are appropriate for kindergarten and upper elementary classrooms.

Music and Poetry

1. Explore different ways of speaking the poem. Use different expressive nuances such as dynamics, tempo, and vocal inflection. Determine what the intended mood or effect of the poem is and try to create this mood with vocal inflection.

2. Find the rhyming words and create special effects to accompany them with body percussion or Orff classroom instruments.

3. Develop awareness of the rhythm of the poem by echo saying, clapping and patting the words. Move to the rhythm of the poem.

4. Develop an *ostinato* to accompany the poem by using important words, phrases, or ideas generated by the poem.

5. Perform the rhythms of the ostinato and words of the poem on classroom instruments as a musical accompaniment. Use single tones on the Orff instruments or pitches from the pentatonic scale.

6. Create special instrumental accompaniments or sound effects for the key words in the poem.

Music and Children's Literature (early childhood)

1. Sing the text. Very often the text of an early childhood book will fit to the tune of a familiar song such as "Shortnin Bread" or "The Wheels on the Bus." *Sol mi* also works well for a melody to some early childhood texts.

2. Sing certain phrases from the text, particularly if they repeat throughout the story. Create a melodic pattern for the phrase based on the pentatonic scale or the descending major scale.

3. Use call and response for question and answers or conversations between characters in the story. The teacher reads the question and the class answers. Again melodic patterns may be used to enhance this activity.

4. Use different instrumental sounds to portray different characters in the story. Use special effects such as tremolos on Orff instruments and maracas to create tension at exciting parts of the plot.

5. Emphasize featured long and short vowel sounds in stories and poetry with movement or instrumental accompaniment.

6. Create special accompaniments or effects for figures of speech like alliteration, simile, and metaphor.

7. Use different percussion instruments for each different punctuation mark in a story.

Music Listening and Language (upper elementary)

Just about any music (preferably art music) with contrasts in tempo, dynamics, and timbre can be used as a stimulus for creative writing projects. Have the children create a plot to accompany the form or major contrasting ideas in a music listening selection. For example, use the beginning of *Rhapsody in Blue* by Gershwin to create a plot and characters. The beginning of Beethoven's *Fifth Symphony* can also generate interesting character and plot descriptions. Have the children write plots with character descriptions and then dramatize their creations with the music as accompaniment.

Listen to a music selection and have the children describe how the music makes them feel, and then most importantly, why does the music make them feel this way. Describing what it is about the music that affects their feelings will encourage increased perception, good thought structure, and clear use of language.

Listen to descriptive music such as Saint Saens' *Carnival of the Animals*, Mussorgsky's *Pictures at an Exhibition*, and Vivaldi's *Four Seasons*. (See Classics for the Classroom) Have the children describe what they hear without giving away the "correct" answer. For example, which animal is this? Why? Or, for the Vivaldi, which season does this represent? Describe why you think it is Fall, Winter, Spring, or Summer. Students could then read the original poems that accompany the *Four Seasons* and create their own. Music can provide a very evocative source for plots, character descriptions, descriptive essays and creative writing.

Music and Social Studies

There are numerous opportunities to include music in the area of social studies or history. Music from different historical periods will enhance student perception of these periods. For instance, the music of Haydn and Mozart was popular during early American history. Also, a composer, William Billings, was one of the signers of the Declaration of Independence. Recordings of his composition, *Chester*, are available from a number of different sources.

Excerpt from Chester

Aaron Copland, perhaps the most accomplished of American composers wrote many compositions that are related to the historical development of America. *Appalachian Spring* includes the popular *Variations on a Shaker Tune*, a famous early American folk tune, *Simple Gifts*, and his *Rodeo* captures the expansiveness of the western frontier.

Excerpt from Simple Gifts

These compositions and others help create the emotional feeling of living during these periods and make the study of history more real for students. Recordings of the music of the revolutionary war and the civil war are now available from a number of different sources. Students can hear early American versions of *Yankee Doodle, Sergeant O'Leary, Gary Owen, The Bonnie Blue Flag, Marching Through Georgia*, and other songs from these wars.

There are many interesting facts about the military music of these periods that students will enjoy. Music was a very important part of military life. For example, from Roman times until the late nineteenth century musicians led troops into battle. During the revolutionary war each company of soldiers had a drummer and a fife player that performed different music throughout the day to signal certain times and duties for the troops. Students will enjoy forming a company of revolutionary soldiers and marching to this spirited music. The famous painting, *The Spirit of 76* by Archibald

M. Willard, depicts the role of the drummer and fife players during the revolutionary war.

The civil war military bands played instruments that pointed behind them. The bands marched in front of the troops so their instruments had to be pointed to the rear. This era of American history has a wealth of music that illustrates the feelings of the time. A careful listening to *When Johnny Comes Marching Home* captures the feelings that both sides of this conflict must have held about the tragedy of the war.

Music can also help to illustrate the social conditions during these periods. The tragedy of slavery is very easily perceived through the work songs and spirituals of Black Americans. Students should hear this music and understand that it became the foundation for much of what is called American music, jazz, blues, and the popular music of today. The following is a sample lesson plan from a fifth grade social studies class about slavery.

Slavery and Spirituals

Objective: To develop an understanding of the development and meaning of the spiritual in black history.

1. Show the video excerpt from the popular movie "Glory" where the freed slaves and born free men sing *Wade in the Water*. Explain that the 54th Regiment was an all-black regiment of soldiers that had been allowed to fight for their freedom and that both former slaves and men who had been born free were included in the regiment.

2. Lead a discussion on why the men are singing the night before battle. Suggest that the music was very powerful and kept spirits high even when times were difficult. Relate this use of music to the life of a slave.

3. Sing the spiritual, *Chatter with the Angels*, with the class. Discuss what meanings may be implied by the words, "I hope to join that band and chatter with the angels all day long."

4. Assignment: Have students pretend they are slaves and are living in the 1800s. Have them write a story, poem, or diary entry about how they would feel and how music might help them feel.

Just about every significant event or period in history has accompanying music that captures the feeling of the times. Often there are folk dances, the Virginia Reel for example, that may also be learned as part of the study of a historical period. The use of music in this way is a very real and valid way to enhance the learning experiences of students.

Social studies often include the study of geography and the people of different lands and cultures. Again, there are many valid opportunities to include music in these studies. Our multicultural society demands that we study the cultures of various peoples. The music of a culture captures the essence of living in that culture. The following is an outline for a unit on Appalachian culture for the fourth grade.

Social Studies
Grade 4

Objective: To acquaint the children with the folk ways and customs of the geographical region of Appalachia.

1.   Geography/Basic History

    A. Exhibit map and discussion
            mountains, hills, rivers, cities, towns
            identify states
            color map
    B. Identify famous people and achievements from area

2.   Culture

    A. Music
        discuss musical instruments
            fiddle
            banjo
            harmonica
            autoharp
            hammer dulcimer
        guest fiddler
        sing *Old Joe Clark*
            circle dance, move in touch hands and out for verse, move to left for each refrain
         play and sing other Appalachian folk songs

    B. Art
            basket weaving
            corn husk dolls
            quilting
            do paper weavings

    C. Folk tales about Appalachia
        Carson, *Stories I Ain't Tole Nobody Yet*
            weather
            mountain life
            family life
            sickness/health
            love/happiness

    D. Occupations
            coal mining
            farming
            guest speaker

Old Joe Clark

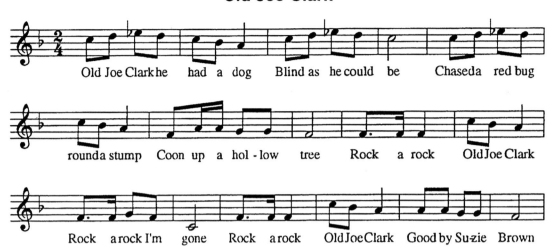

Old Joe Clark he had a dog Blind as he could be Chased a red bug

round a stump Coon up a hol - low tree Rock a rock Old Joe Clark

Rock a rock I'm gone Rock a rock Old Joe Clark Good by Suzie Brown

The music textbook series provide excellent source materials for the music of other cultures and lands. As mentioned earlier, the indexes to the various grade books include categories for the music of different cultures. One text lists folk songs from the following cultures: African, American, Black America, American Indian, Educadoran, English, Flemish, French, German, New Zealand, Portuguese, Puerto Rican, and Spanish. Many are in the original language with accompanying pronunciation guides. The recordings make the use of these materials very practical.The following song is an African call and response song. The teacher sings the call parts (C); the class sings the response (R).

Kye Kye Kule

(An Akan Call-and-Response Exercise Song)

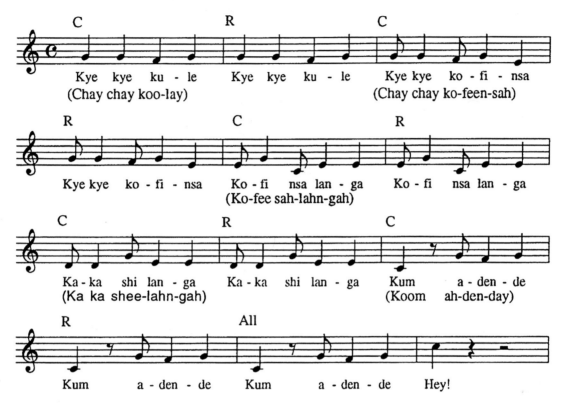

(From: *Let Your Voice be Heard! Songs from Ghana and Zimbabwe*, C. 1986 World Music Press, PO Box 2565, Canbury CT 06813. Used by permission.)

Other Integrative Categories

Some other obvious integrative categories for music include the seasons of the year, holidays, and visual art. More than likely the music specialist will teach students songs about the seasons and holidays as they occur, but the classroom teacher may wish to do a special unit on a season. For example, a unit on fall might include drawings and colorful bulletin boards of the changing colors, stories about things that occur in the fall, and music about fall. In this instance, *Fall* from Vivaldi's *Four Seasons* might be played for the students or even the jazz classic *Autumn Leaves.* The music textbook series include songs for different seasons and holidays often accompanied by poems and colorful pictures of scenes from the different seasons.

There are some very good ways to integrate the visual arts and music. Students may wish to draw or color the shape (contour) and sounds of short orchestral excerpts. Or, the teacher may relate the different periods of art style with the music of the same period. The most obvious connection is between impressionistic painting and impressionistic music. Just about any painting of an outdoor scene by Monet may be combined with a performance of Debussy's *Prelude to the Afternoon of a Faun*. Again, the music textbook series have many suggestions about the combination of music and the visual arts.

Planning and Integration

As mentioned previously, there are many ways to integrate music into the curriculum. For true integration to occur, however, there must be cooperation among the different teachers and specialists of the school faculty. Integration should not be a burden for the classroom teacher or the specialist. Schools may wish to adopt forms like the following to facilitate the curriculum integration process.

The form on the following pages will make integration a lot easier for everyone involved. It will facilitate the planning of the specialty and the classroom teacher. Each will know what is needed in terms of topics, equipment, and vocabulary.

CULTURAL LITERACY IN THE CLASSROOM

Many children may never come in contact with the great achievements of their own cultures. This is especially true in music and art. Children often are not exposed to the great music and art of their culture. As a result, many never develop an accurate sense of their past or their cultures' contribution to human development. They become culturally illiterate. It is here that the classroom teacher can make a valuable contribution. Although the music specialist may attempt to expose children to the great masters of western art music, there is often little time for the repeated exposure necessary to develop understanding and broaden preference. Informal listening in the classroom to a variety of musics can greatly enhance the aesthetic perception and understanding of students and their cultural literacy. If children do not hear Bach, Beethoven, Mozart, and the great jazz players in their schools, they may never hear them.

INTEGRATION FORM
(Classroom Topics —> Specialty Areas)

Specialty Area: _____

Classroom Teacher: _____ Grade: _____

Theme: _____

Dates to be integrated: _____

Topics: _____   Key Vocabulary _____
                _____   _____
                _____   _____
                _____   _____
                _____   _____

I desire the following:

___ Equipment/Supplemental materials to use in my classroom:

     _____
     _____
     _____
     _____

___ Theme/Topics to be reinforced in specialty class:

     _____
     _____
     _____
     _____

___ Assistance from specialty teacher: ____ Planning

_____ Whole Group _____ Small Group _____ Individual

(purpose)   _____
                      _____
                      _____
                      _____

INTEGRATION FORM
(Classroom Topics —> Specialty Areas)

Specialty Area: *Music*

Classroom Teacher: *Mrs. Gray*   Grade: *5*

Theme: *Civil War*

Dates to be integrated: *March 4 and 5*

Topics: *Slavery*   Key Vocabulary   *Spirituals*
                                                             Work songs
        _____   _____
        _____   _____
        _____   _____

I desire the following:

  *   Equipment/Supplemental materials to use in my classroom:

      Cassette player and cassettes of spirituals or work songs
      _____
      _____
      _____

  *   Theme/Topics to be reinforced in specialty class:

      Music and feeling, spirituals, work songs, etc.
      _____
      _____
      _____

  *   Assistance from specialty teacher:

* Planning _____ Whole Group _____ Small Group _____ Individual

  (purpose)

*I need to know of available materials, work songs and spirituals,
that may be performed by the children or listened to on cassettes.*

The following is a very brief annotated list of "classics for the classroom." They may be used for informal listening at the beginning of the day, during quiet times, to accompany busy work, or for special integrated lessons. Recordings of these works are available at most record (now compact disc) stores. As teachers use recordings of the following "classics" they will discover others that they may find appropriate for the classroom.

In accordance with the principles for developing preference, the following classics are mostly fast and all are instrumental. There are many wonderful operas that students should know but opera will take much time and study to be presented effectively to young children. Opera might best be presented by the music specialist.

The following works may be used very easily. The teacher should listen once or twice before attempting to integrate the selections with creative writing or other curriculum projects. Short excerpts may be used when introducing the longer works and the teacher should remember to enthusiastically model preference or acceptance for the music.

Classics for the Classroom

Johann Sebastian Bach (1685 -1750). Bach is one of the greatest composers of all time and certainly the most prolific. He wrote music for just about every combination of instruments and voices except opera. He held a variety of musical positions in Germany which included church organist, court musician, and music director for churches and schools.

Air on a G String (the slow movement from Orchestra Suite No. 3 in D major). *Air on a G String* is one of Bach's most popular and accessible works. It is very good for quiet time or as an accompaniment to quiet individual work. The tempo is slow but there is a "walking pulse" that keeps the piece from being too boring for children.

Brandenburg Concerto No. 2 in F (1st and 3rd movements). The Brandenburg Concertos were written around 1721 and given to a the Margrave of Brandenburg (a German noble, the king's uncle) in Germany. They are virtuoso works. No. 2 has an exciting, high, trumpet part that students will enjoy. The teacher may wish to begin listening with the 3rd movement. It has been very popular and used often in television and movie productions. Many will have heard it before. These are great selections for informal listening as the students enter the classroom in the morning.

Ludwig van Beethoven (1770 - 1827). Beethoven may be the greatest composer ever. He was born in Bonn, Germany and spent much of his time composing in Vienna, Austria. Beethoven's period was the time of George Washington, the French revolution, and Napoleon. His music reflects the turbulent times during which he lived. It is often considered heroic and triumphant. His symphonies, in particular the 3rd, 5th, and 9th represent the highest achievement in instrumental music. They are much too long to be played in their entirety for elementary school classes. However, brief excerpts may serve to illustrate the period that

Beethoven lived in, stimulate creative writing projects, and familiarize the students with one of the greatest composers of all time.

Symphony No. 3 Eroica (1st and 2nd movements). An excerpt (one and a half minutes) from the 1st movement might serve as an illustration of heroic ideals, or heroism. Beethoven is said to have dedicated this symphony to Napoleon, but later withdrew the dedication after Napoleon had himself declared Emperor. The students may discuss the meaning of heroism, historical figures who were heroic and what made them heroic, and how Beethoven's music reflects the period of Washington, Jefferson, and Napoleon. The teacher may wish to contrast the first two minutes of the 2nd movement with the first. The second movement begins with a funeral march.

Symphony No. 5 . (1st, 3rd, and 4th movements). This is Beethoven's most popular and recognized symphony. Many students will already have heard portions of the 1st movement and its famous opening motive. The first three minutes of this movement are a good example of repetition and contrast. Beethoven repeats the famous four note motive throughout the orchestra until the listener thinks that it will never change. Then after the French horn, a flowing new idea brings relief. The students may write a description of these two contrasting ideas or they may invent a plot which follows Beethoven's dramatic opening to this symphony.

The first two minutes of the 3rd movement again feature two contrasting ideas. A very mysterious theme begins in the low strings and is tossed around the orchestra. This is followed by a four note motive very similar to the famous beginning of the 1st movement. These two contrasting ideas alternate for the first two minutes. The students may enjoy writing a plot to follow these contrasts or they may discuss the effects of the two contrasting themes. Is one heroic, another mysterious?

After the opening section of the 3rd movement, Beethoven uses canon (round) technique. The students can easily identify the different instrument entrances. The "round" begins in the low strings followed by the bassoon and violas, and then the violins. This movement ends with the four note motive from the beginning of the movement and moves very mysteriously with the timpani (low pitched drums) into the triumphant theme of the 4th movement. There is no pause between movements. Students will enjoy identifying when the 4th movement begins and describing the effect of moving from the mysterious ending of the 3rd through the first minute of the 4th. This transition from the 3rd to the 4th movements is one of the great achievements in Western music.

Symphony No. 6 The Pastoral. Beethoven often composed outdoors while taking long walks. He named the five movements to this symphony after scenes in the country. They are: (1) Awakening of Cheerful Feelings on Arrival in the Country; (2) Scene by the Brook; (3) Merrymaking of the Country Folk; (4) Storm; and (5) Song of the Shepherds, Joy and Gratitude after the Storm. Walt Disney included this popular symphony in his animated film *Fantasia*, and many students may recognize it, particularly the Storm movement. The 1st, 2nd, 3rd, and 5th movements are very melodious and suitable for background listening or perhaps as the children prepare to leave for the day. They may also serve as accompaniment to drawing nature scenes or for viewing colorful pictures of landscapes. The 2nd movement is over twelve minutes long but it ends with a coda that features the flute, oboe, and clarinet imitating the sounds of the nightingale, quail, and cuckoo.

The 3rd movement makes one think of dancing and merriment and the 4th is obviously a storm. Perhaps students might enjoy drawing a storm scene while listening to this movement or the teacher might have them write in their daily journals what this movement "sounds like" before telling them that Beethoven named it Storm. The Storm calms and the 5th movement begins with the clarinet playing the shepherd's song. The horn follows and then the strings.

Aaron Copland (1900 - 1990). Aaron Copland is the most popular American composer and many consider him to be the greatest American composer. He used American jazz and folk song in his music which gives it a distinctive American sound.

Hoe-Down from *Rodeo* (1942). Rodeo is one of Copland's ballet scores. The plot is about a cowgirl trying to get her man. Hoe-Down is almost four minutes in length and suggests the old fashioned square dance or hoe-down. There are basically three sections with repetition of the main ideas, two square dance tunes, *Bonyparte* and *McLeod's Reel*. The piece is very colorful with many different timbres, piano, and dance like rhythms. The students will really enjoy this work. It may be integrated with studies about the old west or pioneer days or it may be used as energetic good morning music as the students enter the classroom.

Variations on a Shaker Theme from *Appalachian Spring* (1943). Appalachian Spring was originally a ballet written for the Martha Graham Dance Company. Copland was awarded the Pulitzer Prize for its composition. The music is about a pioneer celebration of spring in Pennsylvania in the 1800s. The shaker theme used in the variations is *Simple Gifts*. It has been very popular and many students will recognize it. The theme is introduced by the clarinet then followed by five variations. Copland uses different timbres, dynamics, tempo, and *canon* technique to achieve variety. This piece may be integrated with studies about the pioneer days, Appalachia, or just used for informal listening in the mornings or at other periods during the day. It is about three minutes in length.

Claude Debussy (1862 - 1918). Debussy was born in a small town near Paris and entered the Paris Conservatory of music when he was eleven years old. He is perhaps the most famous of all French composers. He is particularly known for what was called "impressionism" in music which seemed to reflect the style of the popular painters Monet and Renoir. Debussy sought to create images of sound and stimulate the senses and imagination with his music. Even the titles of his works evoke images. Among his works are *Clouds, The Sea, A Sunken Cathedral, Gardens in the Rain,* and *Reflections in the Water*.

Prelude to the Afternoon of a Faun. Debussy was inspired to compose this tone poem by a poem by Mallarme. The poem is about a faun, half man and half goat, who awakens on a lovely afternoon in the forest. This work is too long (about nine minutes) and too slow for directed listening by young children; however, it is a very good example of impressionism and goes well with any impressionistic painting. The students might be encouraged to imagine a deer or faun in a lush green forest as they listen to the first two minutes, or it may serve to illustrate impressionism in music as the students view impressionistic paintings.

George Gershwin (1898 - 1937). George Gershwin is another uniquely American composer. He was born in New York City and spent most of his life there creating music for Broadway. He wrote the music to many musicals and popular songs and attempted to make jazz a legitimate art form. Jazz, ragtime, the blues, and spirituals were often used in his more serious attempts at large musical forms. Many of his popular songs have become jazz standards and his larger works include *Rhapsody in Blue* and the opera, *Porgy and Bess* which includes the popular *Summertime.*

Rhapsody in Blue is much too long (about fourteen minutes) to listen to completely in one setting. It also features periods of solo piano which young students may not listen to attentively. However, the first two minutes include the famous bluesy clarinet solo followed by muted trumpet and then full orchestra. The clarinet and trumpet almost sound like people talking the blues. Students will enjoy this beginning and may enjoy creating a plot to accompany this beginning dialogue section. *Rhapsody in Blue* also may be integrated with studies about the period leading up to WW II. It is very American because of the blues sound and reflects what many have called the jazz age. About nine minutes into the work is the theme often heard on television in an airline commercial. Students should know that this famous commercial music was written by Gershwin, a great American composer.

Edvard Grieg (1843 - 1907). Grieg was a nationalistic composer from Norway. His most famous works are the music from the *Peer Gynt Suite* and his piano concerto.

In the Hall of the Mountain King from *Peer Gynt Suite.* This music was originally written in 1875 as incidental music to a play by Ibsen. *In the Hall of the Mountain King* is very accessible music for young children. As discussed in the sample music lesson in Chapter One, it features one melody repeated with different instruments, dynamic levels, and a gradually increasing tempo. It may be used to identify different instruments, dynamic levels, or changes in tempo. Young children may also enjoy drawing to it or perhaps creating a story while listening. It begins very quietly with the low strings and increases in tempo and orchestration until it is very loud and fast at the end.

Wolfgang Amadeus Mozart (1756-1791). Mozart was probably the greatest musical genius of all time. He and his sister were featured performers in a concert tour of Europe when he was but six years old. He composed his first symphony at eight and his first opera by twelve. The tragic last years of this young genius were depicted in the popular film *Amadeus.* Music came to Mozart almost instantaneously; he composed it in his mind and then just wrote it down. Thus he was able to laugh, talk, and carry on conversations while he composed. His skill was magical. Mozart wrote for virtually every kind of musical organization from solo piano to opera. He was born in Salzburg and he died in Vienna, Austria. Just about any of his works are appropriate for the classroom.

Eine Kleine Nachtmusik (A little night music, 1st and 4th movements). Mozart wrote a number of serenades that were for performance at social gatherings which were very often held out of doors. This string quintet is of that genre. It is very popular; many students will recognize it. The 1st movement is a little over five minutes in length and the 4th is approximately four minutes long. Both would be appropriate for informal listening in the mornings or at other times, perhaps during individual work. The 4th movement is in *rondo* form; the recurring A theme is very easily identified.

Piano Concerto No. 21 in C (K.467). Mozart wrote seventeen piano concertos. No. 21 is one of the most popular. The first movement is about thirteen minutes long and may be used to begin the day or for background listening during busy times. The melody is very accessible and easily remembered. The 2nd movement is about six minutes in length and slow, but it has a steady pulse accompanied by *tripletis* which give it a sense of movement. This movement would do very well for quiet time. The 3rd movement is about seven minutes, up tempo. and easily listened to. Just about all of Mozart's piano concertos are "easy on the ears." For the most part the melodies are very light and carefree. *Piano Concerto No 27 in Bb* (K. 595), Mozart's last, would also work well in the classroom.

Symphony No. 40 in G minor (K. 550, 1st movement). This is probably Mozart's most popular symphony. The 1st movement is about nine minutes long and basically has just two ideas. The first idea which occurs at the very beginning is heard throughout the entire movement. It is very easily identified and followed. This selection is good for informal or background listening just about any time of the day.

Modest Mussorgsky (1839 -1881). Mussorgsky was a Russian composer whose most popular work is probably the symphonic fantasy *Night on Bald Mountain* heard in the Walt Disney film *Fantasia.* Interestingly, Mussorgsky was an amateur musician; he worked as a clerk with the civil service. His music is considered to be very nationalistic, very Russian. His opera, *Boris Godunov* is also very popular as well as the following *Pictures at an Exhibition.*

Pictures at an Exhibition (orchestrated by Ravel). Mussorgsky composed this work for piano. It was later arranged for orchestra by the French composer Ravel. "Pictures" is a collection of pieces which represents the composer viewing the paintings of a friend at an exhibition. It begins with the familiar *Promenade* which is often heard on television. Many students will recognize it. The *Promenade* depicts the composer walking through the exhibition from painting to painting. Ten different paintings are vividly described in sound by the composer.

This selection may be used over a period of time as a stimulus for creative writing or visual art work. The teacher may wish to describe the background of the work and let the students create their own paintings or stories to go with each sound description. After hearing each painting, the students will enjoy comparing their own impressions to the intent of the composer. The *Promenade* is interjected between paintings one and two, two and three, four and five, and eight and nine.

The teacher may begin listening with just the *Promenade* and the *Gnome* followed by the *Promenade* (about five minutes). The final two pictures, *Hut of the Baba Yaga* and *The Great Gate of Kiev,* (about nine minutes) will be very popular with students. Ravel used the full range of orchestra timbres to create a stirring climax.

Johann Pachelbel (1653 - 1706). Pachelbel was born in Nuremburg, Germany and was an early influence on J. S. Bach. He held positions as court or church organist in many cities throughout Germany. Many of his compositions are for organ.

Pachelbel's Canon was originally written for organ but has become very popular as an arrangement for strings. It has been used in movies and is heard quite frequently on radio and television. It's about five minutes long and may work very well for quiet time or as informal listening during individual work.

Richard Strauss (1864 - 1949). Richard Strauss was an early twentieth century German composer and celebrated conductor who is most remembered for his symphonic poems and operas. His symphonic poems are both philosophical and descriptive in that he attempted to represent philosophical ideals as well as describe characters and scenes. His most popular work is the symphonic poem *Till Eulenspiegel's Merry Pranks.*

Thus Spake Zarathustra (introduction). Zarathustra was one of Strauss's more philosophical symphonic poems but its introduction has been applied very descriptively in a number of different situations. Many will recognize it as the theme from *2001 A Space Odyssey*. The introduction is very dramatic, powerful, and about two minutes long. Strauss supposedly meant it to signify the sunrise; however, it has been used in a variety of different situations to represent power and strength. For example, it is often used at athletic contests. Teachers may wish to have students describe the feelings created by this powerful work or perhaps the teacher might use it as a fanfare to announce high achievers or significant figures from history.

Camille Saint-Saens (1835 - 1921). Saint-Saens was a popular French composer who wrote for almost all combinations of instruments and voices. His music is considered distinctly French. His most popular works are the following.

Carnival of the Animals - This popular selection was written for two pianos and chamber ensemble. The work is a collection of short sound depictions of various animals such as the *Royal March of the Lions, Tortoises, The Elephant,* and *The Swan.* There are fourteen short movements from about thirty seconds to three minutes in length. Young children will enjoy trying to identify the animals or in some instances, like *The Elephant,* moving like the animals.

Dance Macabre - This is a short symphonic poem about Death, a fiddler, playing for a dance of spirits and skeletons in a graveyard. The piece begins with the clock (harp) striking twelve for midnight. Then Death, the fiddler, tunes up his fiddle and plays for the spirits. There are two basic melodies that represent the dancing of the skeletons and the sad spirits. Later the wind blows and the cock crows (oboe) to signal dawn and the skeletons and spirits go back to sleep. As mentioned previously, this is definitely a Halloween selection. Students may enjoy drawing a Halloween scene as they listen, or they may wish to dramatize the story with costumes and movement. Macabre is about seven minutes long.

Bedrich Smetana (1924 - 1884). Smetana was a Czech composer of the nineteenth century. His most popular works are the opera, *The Bartered Bride,* and the collection of tone poems, *My Vlast* (my country), from which *The Moldau* is often performed.

The Moldau (from *My Vlast*). *My Vlast* is a collection of six tone poems about Smetana's country, Bohemia, in what is now Czechoslovakia. The second tone poem describes the river, the Moldau, from its beginning as a murmuring brook, as it flows by a village where a festival is taking place, past a forest and a hunt, and on by a large castle. This selection might work well as a stimulus for a creative writing project. Smetana paints exciting sound pictures of the different parts of the country as the stream passes. *The Moldau* is about six minutes in length.

Igor Stravinsky (1882 - 1971). Many consider Stravinsky to be the greatest and most influential composer of the twentieth century. He was born in Russia, lived in Paris, California, and New York. He used many elements in his music from Russian folk song to jazz rhythms. He composed for large orchestras, chamber ensembles, and solo instruments. One of his works, *The Rite of Spring,* caused a riot at its first performance.

The Firebird Suite (*Lullaby* and *Finale*). This is probably Stravinsky's most popular work. It was written for a ballet in Paris in 1910. The ballet is a Russian legend about a magic Firebird who helps a young prince overcome the evil of a demonic magician. The *Lullaby* is a very mysterious piece which features the bassoon and harp. It could serve as a stimulus for creative writing, drawing, or perhaps as an accompaniment to dramatize a mysterious story or poem. It is about four minutes in length and leads directly into the *Finale* which is begun by the French horn. The *Finale* includes a variety of timbres and special effects. It is a very dynamic and uplifting work that builds to a moving climax. The shift in mood from the *Lullaby* to the end of the *Finale* will be enjoyed by the students and they may wish to create a plot to illustrate the dynamic shift and build up of emotions. The *Lullaby* and *Finale* together are about eight minutes long.

Antonio Vivaldi (1678- 1741). Vivaldi spent most of his life in Venice where he was trained for the priesthood and music. He was employed as a conductor, composer, teacher, and general superintendent of music at the Conservatory of Pieta in Venice. Vivaldi wrote many operas and music for the church but he is most remembered for his instrumental music, in particular, his concertos, of which he wrote about 450.

The Four Seasons (*Spring*). The Four Seasons are four violin concertos that Vivaldi wrote to represent the four seasons. Each concerto describes certain aspects of the season that it depicts. For example, *Spring* is accompanied by the following description.

ALLEGRO
     Spring has come
Bird song
     and joyfully the birds welcome it with happy song.
The brooks murmur
     while the streams flow gently murmuring to the breathing of the breezes.
Thunder
     Thunder and lightning cloak the sky with black, heralding a storm.
Bird song
     Then when they are silent the birds once again take up their harmonious song.

LARGO
The sleeping goatherd
The murmuring of the leaves and plants
The barking dog
And here, in a pleasant, flowery meadow, the leaves and the plants murmuring gently,
     the goatherd sleeps, his faithful dog by his side.

ALLEGRO
Pastoral dance
     To the festive sound of the rustic bagpipe nymphs and shepherds dance to Spring,
     brilliantly appearing.

Students will enjoy following the scenic depictions as they listen to the music or *Spring* may be played for informal listening in the mornings or afternoons. It is very spirited and upbeat and probably the most popular of the *Four Seasons*. The other concertos are also appropriate for the classroom. *Summer* includes the cuckoo and turtledove, *Autumn* - a peasant song, dance, and hunt, and *Winter* - walking and falling on ice.

Jazz Classics

Jazz may be more difficult to use for background or informal listening. The great jazz players like Louis Armstrong and Charlie Parker were such great improvisers that their music may be too complex for elementary age school children. Still, students should be familiar with some of the great jazz innovators. In particular, Black Americans may be unaware of their great heritage in American music. The greatest jazz players, Louis Armstrong, Charlie Parker, Miles Davis, and John Coltrane, were Black Americans and their music greatly influenced all of today's popular and serious music.

Virtually any recording by Louis Armstrong (1900 - 1971) or Charlie Parker (1920 - 1955) will demonstrate the greatness of these two giants of jazz. Parker was like Mozart in that he was extremely gifted and is perhaps the most influential jazz player of all time. Unfortunately, the recording quality of his records make them difficult to appreciate. Elementary age children may not be able to get beyond the poor quality of sound of his records.

The following two albums were very influential in jazz and popular music. They greatly influenced other jazz players and the music that they composed. Although the music is again complex, the improvisatory setting is accessible and such that young children may be able to remember the tunes and arrangements and thus develop the familiarity necessary for increased understanding and enjoyment.

Time Out—The Dave Brubeck Quartet (1960). Columbia Records. This classic jazz album includes the jazz classics *Take Five* and *Blue Rondo a la Turk*. Both pieces have very accessible melodies and the solos by Paul Desmond (saxophone) are light and tuneful. This album caused quite a stir in the jazz world because of Brubeck's experimentation with different meters. *Take Five* is in a five meter (3 + 2) and *Blue Rondo a la Turk* alternates between nine (2 + 2 + 2 + 3) and four (common duple meter). The *rondo* form of a recurring theme is also very easy to identify. The students will enjoy these recordings in the mornings or afternoons. The recording quality is excellent and the album has been reissued as a compact disc. The popular *Take Five* might serve as a signal for break time.

Kind of Blue—The Miles Davis Quintet (1959). Columbia Records. Miles Davis (1926 - 1991), one of the most influential jazz players, perhaps second only to Charlie Parker, changed the harmonic language of jazz with this album. The classic *So What* from this album utilizes a harmonic scheme based upon modal scales rather than changing chords. This album also includes two of the greatest saxophone players, Cannonball Adderly and John Coltrane. Coltrane went on to become a very innovative and influential player in his own right. The students will enjoy *So What*. If they listen carefully they will be able to identify the title of the tune. The bass performs a solo and the horns answer "so what." *All Blues*, also on this album, has become a jazz standard. It will work for quiet time. *Kind of Blue* has also been reissued on compact disc.

Chapter Summary

Music is one of the most powerful elements in contemporary society. It is used for political, ceremonial, commercial, and religious purposes. It can also be used in education. In particular the classroom teacher may utilize music throughout the day and within the curriculum to heighten the learning experiences of students. This will not only contribute to the success of the teacher and the students but it will also contribute to the music specialist's efforts in the development of music skills and aesthetic sensitivity.

The classroom teacher may use music throughout the day for greetings, routine activities, and to end the day. The teacher may also integrate music with other subjects in the curriculum or use it to support the study of an organizing topic or concept. Music can illustrate concepts in almost any discipline. It works particularly well with language arts, history, and cultural studies. When music is integrated it should enhance the education experience, not just entertain. Superficial attempts to integrate music with other subjects may actually distract students and place unnecessary burden on the teacher.

Class Activities

1. Make a collection of greeting songs. See the music textbook series.

2. Compose some original songs and chants for routine activities such as going to lunch, etc.

3. Modify some familiar songs to teach a basic skill or math concept.

4. Select a poem, nursery rhyme, or a childhood fable and dramatize it with musical sound effects and melodies.

5. Listen to Smetana's *The Moldau* and Mussorgsky's *Pictures at an Exhibition*. Create an original story to accompany each. Draw a picture of the musical features of each.

6. Peruse the music textbooks for integrative suggestions. Evaluate them for their practicality and value.

7. Make a list of songs and recordings for music from other cultures.

8. Make a list of songs and recordings for use with studies about the colonial and revolutionary periods and the civil war.

9. Listen to Copland's *Hoe-Down* from *Rodeo* and *Variations on a Shaker Tune* from *Appalachian Spring*. Discuss the American aspects of each and how they might be integrated into the curriculum.

10. Make a collection or list of recordings to be used for informal listening (in the mornings) and quiet times.

SUGGESTED RECORDINGS

Appalachian Folk

"Doc Watson sings Songs for Little Pickers" Doc Watson, 1990 Sugar Hill Records, P O Box 4040 Duke Station, Durham, NC 27706

Early Childhood and Basic Skills

"On the Move" Greg and Steve, Youngheart Records. P. O. Box 27784, Los Angeles, 90027.
"We All Live Together" Volumes 1 through 4. Greg and Steve, Youngheart Records. P. O. Box 27784, Los Angeles90027
"Learning Basic Skills Through Music" Hap Palmer, Educational Activities, Inc. Box 392, Freeport, NY 11520.
"Witches Brew" Hap Palmer, Educational Activities, Inc. Box 392, Freeport, NY 11520.
"Singable Songs for the Very Young" Raffi, A & M Records, Inc. P O Box 118, Hollywood, CA 90028.

Revolutionary and Civil War

"The Spirit of 76: Music for Fifes and Drums" Frederick Fennell, Mercury Records Golden Imports (Stereo SRI 75048).
"Music of the Civil War" Eastman Wind Ensemble, Frederick Fennell Mercury Records Golden Imports (Stereo SRI 2-77011).
"The Confederacy" by Richard Bales, Columbia Records, 666 Fifth Ave. P. O. Box 4450, NY 10101-4450.
"The Union" by Richard Bales, Columbia Records, 666 Fifth Ave. P. O. Box 4450, NY 10101-4450.
"The Civil War" Original Soundtrack Recording, Elektra Nonesuch (9 79256-2), Elektra Entertainment, a division of Warner Communications Inc. 75 Rockefeller Plaza, NY 10019.

Music Textbooks

Beethoven, J., Davidson, J., & Nadon-Gabrion, C. (1991).*World of music*. Morristown, NJ: Silver Burdett and Ginn.
Boardman, E. & Andress, B. (1984). *The music book*. New York: Holt, Rinehart, and Winston, Publishers.

Crook, E. Reimer, B., & Walker, D. (1985). *Silver Burdett Music: Centennial edition.* Morristown, NJ: Silver Burdett Company.

Staton, B., Staton, M., Davidson, M., & Snyder, S. (1988). *Music and you.* New York: Macmillan Publishing Company.

REFERENCES

Carson, J. (1991). *Stories I ain't told nobody yet.* New York: Theater Communications Group.

Cherry, Lynne. (1990). *The great kapok tree. A tale of the Amazon rain forest.* New York: Gulliver Books, Harcourt Brace Jovanovich, Publishers.

Choksy, L., & Brummitt, D. (1987). *120 Singing Games and Dances for Elementary Schools.* Englewood Cliffs, NJ. : Prentice-Hall, Inc.

Giles, M. (1991). A music and art program to promote emotional health in elementary school children. *Journal of Music Therapy 28*(3), 135-148.

Mark, M. L. (1986). *Contemporary music education* (2nd ed.) New York: Schirmer Books.

Hanshumaker, J. (1986). The effects of music and other arts instruction on reading and math achievement. *Update: The Applications of Research in Music Education, 4*(2), 10-11.

Rylant, C. (1985). *The relatives came.* New York: Bradberg Press.

Shanahan, T. (1991). New literacy goes to school: Whole language in the classroom. *Educational Horizons 69*(3), 141-151.

Stewart, E. L. (1991). Using music in the classroom. *Mathematics Teacher, 84*(8), 632.

Warren, J. (1983). *Piggyback songs.* Everett, WA: Warren Publishing House.

Wolff, K. L. (1978). The nonmusical outcomes of music education: a review of the literature. *Bulletin of the Council for Research in Music Education, 55*, 1-27.

APPENDIX

Common Key Signatures

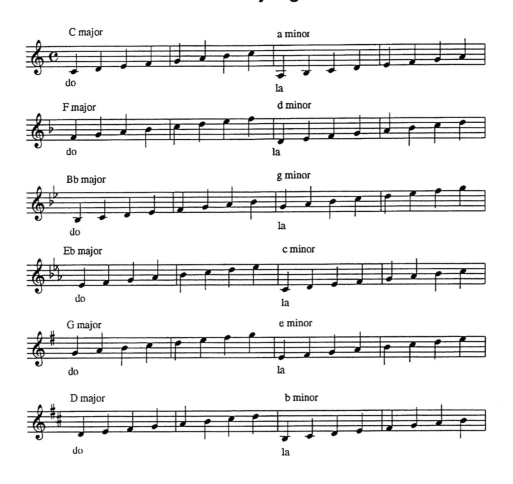

The Treble Clef
(Pitch Names)

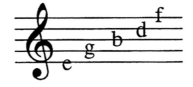

FOLK SONGS

1.	Teddy Bear	sm, slsm, ti ti ta ti ti ta
2.	Peas Porridge	sm, sd, ta ti ti ta sh
3.	This Old Man	sms, ti tiri, tiri ti, tiritiri ta
4.	Oliver Twist	sm, smlsm, compound meter
5.	Acka Backa	slsm, ti ti
6.	Blue Bird	slsm, ta ti ti ta ta
7.	Kookaburra	slsm, tiritiri ti tiri
8.	Zero	msls, dsls, ti ti
9.	Hot Cross Buns	mrd, ta ta ta sh
10.	Hop Old Squirrel	mrd, ta ta ta sh
11.	Old King Glory	mrd, sd, octave**, ta ta timri timri
12.	Sally Go Round the Sun	dms, mrd, tripleti
13.	Liza Jane	mrd, lsms, syncopa ta
14.	Charlie Over The Ocean	drm, ds, timri, tripleti
15.	Jim Along Josie	smrms, smrd
16.	Row Your Boat	drm, dsmd, compound meter
17.	Button	drms, rs, md, ti ti ti ti ta ta
18.	Bow Wow Wow	dm, slsmd, ta ta ta sh
19.	Rocky Mountain	dm, dmsl
20.	Grandma Grunts	dm, ds
21.	24 Robbers	dm, sld
22.	Down Came a Lady	dm, mrd, ti riri, tiri ti
23.	Can't Dance Josey	d, mrms, rdls, tiritiri
24.	Hambone	mdldm, ti tiri tiritiri ti ti ta
25.	Who's That	ds, rmrd
26.	Clapping Land	ds, lsfmrd, timri ti ti
27.	Ding Dong	dsls, tiritiri
28.	A Ram Sam Sam	sd, tiritiri
29.	Chatter With The Angels	dls, sld, tiritiri, ta timri
30.	Old Brass Wagon	dls, sld, tiritiri, timri titi titi
31.	Old Lady Sittin In The Dining Room	dls, dms, lsmd, mdls, cut time***
32.	Punchinella	dsls, syncopa
33.	When The Train Comes Along	ldm, ta timri
34.	Hey Ho, Nobody's Home	lslm, tiritiri, timri
35.	When Johnny Comes Marching Home	mltd, compound meter

36. Hear Ye The Wind Is Rising   lrfl, sdms, ta timri, dorian mode****
37. Skin and Bones   ldrl, mrdl, compound meter

Primary melody and rhythm patterns are given. (More melodic and rhythmic analyses are given with each song.)

** An octave is the interval of an eighth (in this song, high sol to low sol)
*** Each note is one half of its original value, i.e. ta ta equals ti ti and ti ti ti ti equals tiritiri
**** Home tone or tonic is re

1. Teddy Bear (sm, slsm, smr, mrd) (titi ta titi ta)

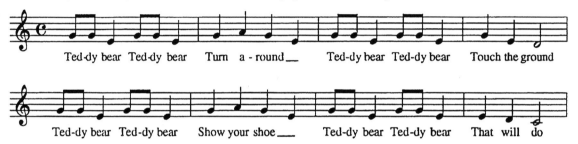

2nd verse Teddy Bear Teddy Bear, Go up stairs, Teddy Bear Teddy Bear, Say your prayers, Teddy Bear Teddy Bear, Turn out the light, Teddy Bear Teddy Bear, Say good night.

Movement Children do actions to words in song (turn around, touch ground, show shoe, open hands to side, etc.)

2. Peas Porridge Hot (sms, sd) (ta titi ta sh)

Movement Children sit Indian style across from partner. During first two phrases, pat thighs, clap hands, clap partners hands, and clap hands. During second two phrases, pat thighs, clap hands, partners clap right hands, clap own hands, partners clap left hands, and clap own hands. Young children may not be able to do cross clapping (partners right and left) easily.

3. This Old Man (sms, sd, drmfs, mrd) (ti tiri, tiri ti, tiritiri ta)

Other Verses This old man, He played two-shoe; three-knee; four-door; five-hive; six-sticks; seven-heaven; eight-gate; nine-vine; ten-hen.

Movement Children count with fingers, roll hands on rolling home.

4. Oliver Twist (sm, smlsm) (compound meter)

Movement Teacher does movement for children to copy then everyone touches knees, toes, claps and turns around.

5. Acka Backa (slsm) (titi, ta ta ta-ah)

Movement A choosing game. Point to different child on each pulse. One who is chosen on "you" is it.

6. Bluebird (slsm, mrdmd) (ta titi ta ta, ta-ah titi titi)

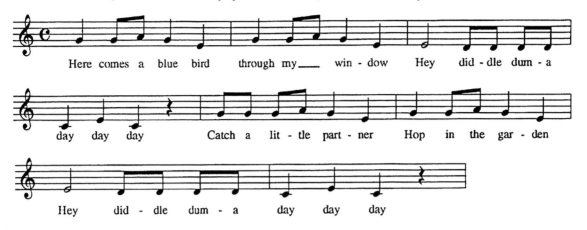

Movement In a circle children hold hands up high to make windows. The child who is the blue-bird flies like a bird in and out the windows. On "catch a little partner," the bluebird chooses someone and they hold hands facing to "hop in the garden" (the circle). The partner is now the new bluebird.

7. Kookaburra (slsm, md, round) (tiritiri ti tiri titi titi, ta tiritiri ta)

Second Verse Kookaburra sits on the old gum tree, Eating all the gum drops he could see, Laugh Kookaburra laugh, Kookaburra gay your life must be.

8. Zero (msls, dsls, mrd, mdld) (titi ta titi, ta ta titi)

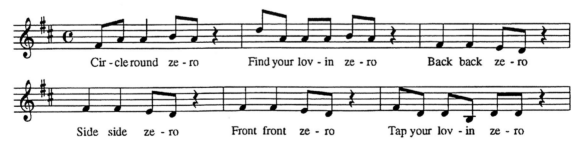

Movement Children stand facing in circle patting thighs as they sing. The child who is "it" dances around the circle until on the words "back back" the child ("it") bumps rears with a partner, on "side side," bumps sides, on "front front," claps partner's hands, on "tap" taps partner's shoulders. The partner now follows "it" outside the circle. Two partners are then chosen for the movements. This continues until all the children are chosen.

9. Hot Cross Buns (mrd, drm) (ta ta ta sh, titi titi titi titi)

Hot cross buns Hot cross buns One a pen-ny two a pen-ny Hot cross buns

10. Hop Old Squirrel (mrd, mr) (ta ta ta sh, titi ta titi ta)

Hop old squirrel Ei-dle-dum ei-dle-dum Hop old squirrel Ei-dle-dum de

Hop old squirrel Ei-dle-dum ei-dle-dum Hop old squirrel Ei-dle-dum de

Movement Children hop individually to pulse.

11. Old King Glory (mrd, sd, ss - octave*) (ta ta timri timri)

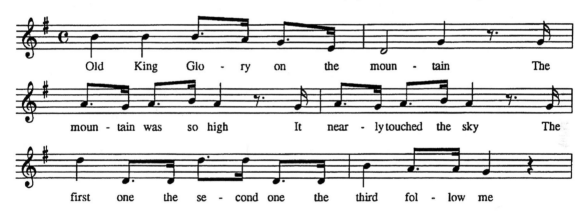

Old King Glo - ry on the moun - tain The

moun - tain was so high It near - ly touched the sky The

first one the se - cond one the third fol - low me

Movement Children face in a circle and pat, clap, clap partners hands to each side, and clap own hands to the pulse. The child who is "it" dances around the circle and on "first, second, third" touches children to join in the line and follow around the circle. New members of line must copy silly movements of "it" as they dance and choose three more line members. Game continues until all children are chosen.

* An octave is an interval of an eighth. In this song from high sol to low sol.

12. Sally Go Round The Sun (dms, mrd, round) (tripleti, timri)

Sal - ly go round the sun   Sal - ly go round the sun

Sal - ly go round the sun - shine   ev - ry af - ter noon

13. Liza Jane (mrd, lsms, dsls) (syn co pa ta, tum ti)

Come my love and go with me   Lil Li - za Jane

Come my love and go with me   Lil Li - za Jane

Oh   E - li - za   Lil   Li - za   Jane

Oh   E - li - za   Lil   Li - za   Jane

Other Verses I gotta house in Baltimore, Lil Liza Jane, Street car runs right by my door, Lil Liza Jane. Oh Eliza, Lil Liza Jane, Oh Eliza, Lil Liza Jane. I gotta house in Baltimore, Lil Liza Jane, Brand new carpet on my floor, Lil Liza Jane. Oh Eliza, Lil Liza Jane, Oh Eliza, Lil Liza Jane. I gotta house in Baltimore, Lil Liza Jane, Golden knocker on my door, Lil Liza Jane. Oh Eliza, Lil Liza Jane, Oh Eliza, Lil Liza Jane.

14. Charlie Over The Ocean (drm, ds) (timri, tripleti)

Char - lie o - ver the o - cean   Char - lie o - ver the o - cean

Char - lie o - ver the sea   Char - lie o - ver the sea   Char - lie caught a big fish

Char - lie caught a big fish   Can't catch me   Can't catch me

Movement A circle chase game. Leader (who's it) sings first phrase then class echos througout song as leader runs around outside circle. On "fish" leader tags someone in the circle who then tries to catch leader before leader completes circle back to original position.

15. Jim Along Josie (smrs, smrd) (titi ta)

Hey   come   a - long   Jim   a - long   Jo - sie

Hey   come   a - long   Jim   a - long   Joe

Other Verses Walk, Come along Jim along Josie, Walk, Come along Jim along Joe, Step, Turn, Hop, etc.

Movement Wave on Hey, step in place, turn in place, hop in place, etc.

16. Row Your Boat (drm, dsmd, sfmrd) (compound meter)

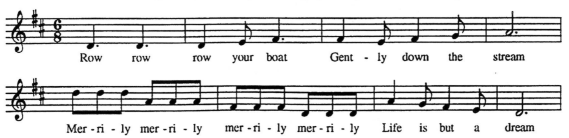

Row   row   row   your boat   Gent - ly down the   stream

Mer - ri - ly mer - ri - ly   mer - ri - ly mer - ri - ly   Life is but a   dream

17. Button (drms, rs, md, lsd) (titi titi ta ta)

But - ton you must wan - der wan - der wan - der

But - ton you must wan - der ev - ry where

Bright eyes will find you Sharp eyes will find you

But - ton you must wan - der ev - ry where

18. Bow Wow Wow (dm, slsmd, mrd) (ta ta ta sh, titi titi titi ta)

Bow wow wow   Whose dog art thou?   Lit-tle Tom-my Tuc-ker's dog   Bow wow wow

Movement Partners stand facing and stamp alternating feet on "Bow wow wow," shake finger in scolding manner on "Whose dog art thou," hold hands and turn around (trade places) on "Little Tommy Tucker's dog," and stamp feet again on "Bow wow wow."

19. Rocky Mountain (dm, dms, lsmd, mrd, mrdr, dmsl)

Roc - ky moun - tain roc - ky moun - tain roc - ky moun - tain high

When you're on that roc - ky moun-tain hang your head and cry Do do do do

do re-mem-ber me Do do do do do re-mem-ber me

Second Verse Stormy ocean, Stormy ocean, Stormy ocean wide, When you're on that stormy ocean, Hang your head and cry. Do do do do etc.

20. Grandma Grunts (dm, ds, mrd) (ta ta ta titi, titi ta ta-ah)

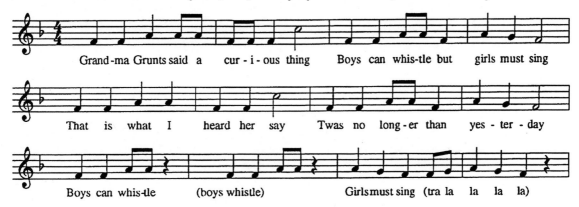

Grand-ma Grunts said a cur-i-ous thing Boys can whis-tle but girls must sing

That is what I heard her say Twas no long-er than yes-ter-day

Boys can whis-tle (boys whistle) Girls must sing (tra la la la la)

21. Twenty Four Robbers (dm, sld, mrd) (titi ti tiri titi ta, tiri ti, tiritiri)

Not last night but the night be-fore Twen-ty four rob-bers at my door

O-pened the door and let one in Hit-em on the head with a rol-lin pin

Other Verses I picked up my frying pan, Shoulda seen the way those robbers ran, Some ran east and some ran west, Some jumped over the cuckoo's nest.

(The melody for Twenty Four Robbers is from Chatter With The Angels by Shirley W. McRae, Copyright 1980 MMB Music, Inc., Saint Louis)

22. Down Came A Lady (dm, mrd) (ti tiri, tiri ti)

Down came a la-dy down came two Down came old Dan-iel's wife dressed in blue

23. Can't Dance Josie (d, mrms, rdls, lsmrd) (tiritiri)

Chic-ken on a fence post   Can't dance Jo-sie   Chic-ken on a fence post   Can't dance Jo-sie

Chic-ken on   a fence post   Can't dance Jo - sie   Hel - lo Su - sie   Brown-ie oh!

Movement Alternate pat rhythm of "Chicken on the fence post" on thighs, clap hands on "Can't dance," clap partner's hands on "Josie," link arms and swing your partner on "Hello Susie Brownie Oh!"

24. Hambone (mdldm, mdldrd) (ti tiri tiritiri ti ti ta)

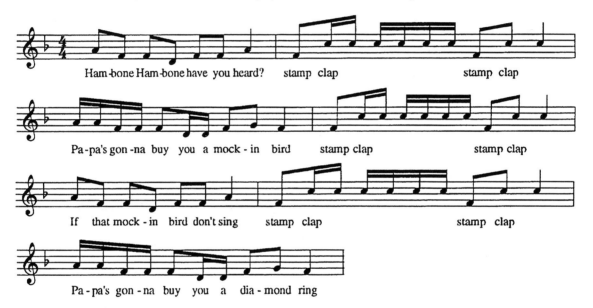

Ham-bone Ham-bone have you heard?   stamp clap   stamp clap

Pa-pa's gon-na buy you a mock - in bird   stamp clap   stamp clap

If   that mock - in bird don't sing   stamp clap   stamp clap

Pa - pa's gon - na buy you a dia - mond ring

Other Verses If that diamond ring don't shine, Papa'a gonna take you to the five and dime, Hambone Hambone where you been, Around the world and I'm going again, Hambone walk and Hambone talk, Hambone eat with a shovel and a fork, Hambone Hambone by the fence, Haven't seen my Hambone since.

25. Who's That (ds, rmrd, rmd) (ta-ah)

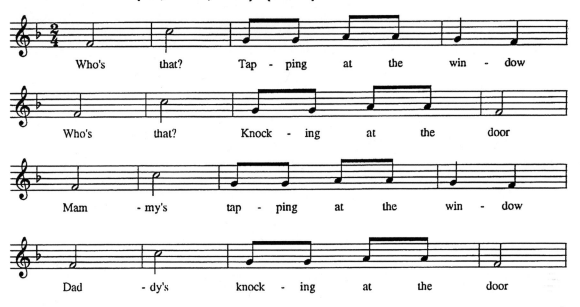

Who's that? Tap - ping at the win - dow

Who's that? Knock - ing at the door

Mam - my's tap - ping at the win - dow

Dad - dy's knock - ing at the door

26. Clapping Land (ds, lsfmrd, sltd) (timri)

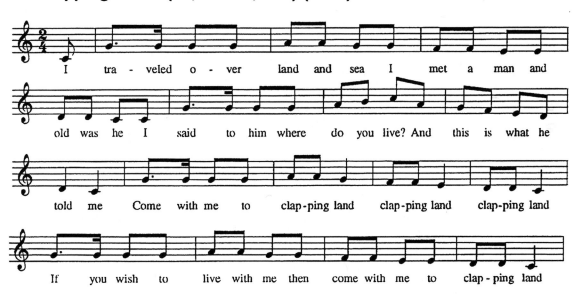

I tra - veled o - ver land and sea I met a man and

old was he I said to him where do you live? And this is what he

told me Come with me to clap-ping land clap-ping land clap-ping land

If you wish to live with me then come with me to clap - ping land

Other Verses Come with me to stamping land, hopping land, walking land, etc.
Movement Children do clapping, stamping, etc. on those words.

27. Ding Dong (dsls, mrmd, ds, round) (tiritiri ta, tiritiri titi)

28. A Ram Sam Sam (sd, md, sm, round) (tiritiri)

29. Chatter With The Angels (dls, sld, mrd, dms) (tiritiri titi, ti tiri titi, ta timri titi titi)

30. Old Brass Wagon (dls, sld) (tiritiri timri titi titi)

Cir-cle to the left   the old brass wa-gon   Cir-cle to the left   the old brass wa-gon

Cir - cle to the left   the old brass wa - gon   you're the one my dar - lin

31. Old Lady Sittin in the Dining Room
(dls, dms, lsmd, mdls, cut time*)

Old   la-dy sit-tin in the   din-ing room   Sit - tin   by   the   fire___

Her   foot slipped and   she   fell down___   Rise   up   high-er and   high-er

*Each note is one half its original value, i.e. ta ta equals ti ti and ti ti ti ti equals tiritiri

32. Punchinella (dsls, sltd) (syncopa)

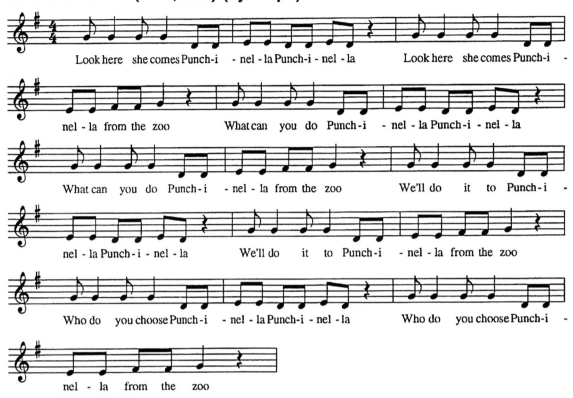

Look here she comes Punch-i - nel - la Punch-i - nel - la   Look here she comes Punch-i -

nel - la from the zoo   What can you do Punch-i - nel - la Punch-i - nel - la

What can you do Punch-i - nel - la from the zoo   We'll do it to Punch-i -

nel - la Punch-i - nel - la   We'll do it to Punch-i - nel - la from the zoo

Who do you choose Punch-i - nel - la Punch-i - nel - la   Who do you choose Punch-i -

nel - la from the zoo

Movement Circle formation with Punchinella in the middle. Children in circle sing first phrase and pat thighs. Punchinella dances/skips around in circle. On "What can you do" Punchinella creates a movement in place that the circle has to imitate on "We'll do it to." On "Who do you choose" Punchinella covers her eyes with one hand and points with the other as she turns around slowly in the circle. At the end of the phrase, the person she is pointing to becomes the new Punchinella.

33. When The Train Comes Along   (ldm, mrdl, rdl) (timri ta, ti tiri)

When the train comes a - long When the train comes a -

long I'm gon-na meet you at the sta-tion when the train comes a - long

34. Hey Ho, Nobody's Home (lslm, mrdtl, round)
(ti tiri ta, tiritiri ta, timri, timri)

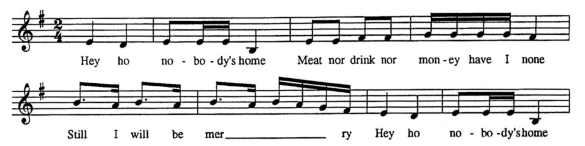

Hey ho no - bo - dy's home   Meat nor drink nor mon - ey have I none

Still I will be mer_____ ry Hey ho no - bo -dy's home

35. When Johnny Comes Marching Home (mltd, compound meter)

When John - ny comes march - ing home a - gain hur - rah_____ hur - rah_____ We'll

give him a heart - y wel - come then hur - rah_____ hur - rah_____ The

men will cheer__ the boys will shout the la - dies they__ will all turn out And we'll

all feel gay when John - ny comes march - ing home_____

36. Hear Ye The Wind Is Rising (lrfl, sdms, dorian mode**) (ta timri)

Hear ye the wind is ris - ing   Hear ye the wind is ris - ing

Hear ye the wind is ris - ing ear - ly in the morn - ing

Second Verse Heave ho and pull the anchor - - Early in the morning.
** Re is home tone or tonic.

37. Skin And Bones (ld, mrdl) (compound meter)

GLOSSARY OF SELECTED MUSICAL TERMS

Arco—To use the bow (pull and push the bow across the strings) when playing the string instruments.

Bordun—An ostinato of *do* and *sol* to accompany pentatonic music. Used in the Orff process.

Cadence—A resting point or pause in music often created by the movement from *sol* to *do*.

Canon—A compositional technique where the melody overlaps with itself. Similar to a round.

Chord—Three or more tones sounded simultaneously.

Chromatic Scale—All half steps. If one were to play all the notes (black and white) within an octave on the keyboard without skipping.

Coda—A special ending. Often used in the Orff process.

Descant—A second melody to accompany the primary melody. Usually at a higher pitch.

Flat—b To lower a pitch by a half step.

Half step—The smallest interval in Western music. To go from one pitch to the next without skipping. For example from c to c sharp.

Homophonic—One melody accompanied by harmony.

Interval—The distance between two pitches. From *do* to *sol* is an interval of a fifth.

Introduction—A special beginning to a piece of music.

Modulation—To change tonalities. To change scales, to change *do*.

Octave—An interval of eight. From low *do* to high *do* (or *sol* to *sol* etc.)

Ostinato—A repeated pattern in music. Often used in elementary music to accompany chants and simple songs.

Phrase—A complete musical thought, a musical sentence.

Pizzicato—To pluck the strings of the string instruments.

Polyphonic—More than one melody simultaneously.

Scale—A sequence of tones arranged in ascending or descending order.

Sharp—# To raise a pitch by a half step.

Time Signature—The numbers at the beginning of a song that indicate the meter. For example, 3/4 indicates triple meter, 2/4 duple, and 6/8 compound.

Tonality—The scale a song is based upon, the home tone, *do* for major tonalities, *la* for minor.

Triad—Three tones sounded simultaneously (a chord) in intervals of three.

Unison—All voices or instruments sounding the same pitch.

Whole Step—To move from one pitch to the next by skipping the half step. For example, c to d skips c#, *do* to *re* is a whole step.

SUBJECT INDEX

A

accent(s)18, 23, 26, 28, 58
action songs 66
aesthetic education 3, 4, 15, 109
aesthetic experience 5, 55, 57, 98, 99
aesthetic perception 17
aesthetic reaction 8, 14, 44, 48, 54
aesthetic response 43, 50, 61, 69
aesthetic reward 77
aesthetic sensitivity 3, 4, 7, 14, 15, 43, 55, 155
Air on a G String 116, 147
alto 53
Appalachian Spring 48, 49, 56, 139, 149, 156
arco 52
Armstrong, Louis 154
art music 7, 8, 15, 33, 77, 138, 144
artistic properties 3, 7, 14, 17
aural perception 7, 33
autoharp (s) 40, 41, 42, 50, 72

B

Bach, Johann Sebastian 5, 7, 116, 130, 144, 147
baritone 53
bass 53
bassoon 52
Beethoven Symphony No. 3 Eroica 148
Beethoven Symphony No. 5 148
Beethoven Symphony No. 6 The Pastoral 148
Beethoven's *Fifth Symphony* 43, 138
Beethoven, Ludwig van 8, 111, 144, 147, 148
Billings, William 139
binary form 10, 12, 45, 48, 49, 121
body percussion 51, 76, 96, 105, 122, 127, 137

bordun 90, 93, 94, 95
Brandenburg Concerto No. 2 in F 147
brass instruments 52
Britten, Benjamin 48, 51, 54

C

cadence 44, 45
call charts 99
canon 91, 92, 148, 149
Carnival of the Animals 127, 138, 152
cello 52
child development 59, 60, 61, 78
chord (s) 40, 41, 42, 55
chromatic scale 31
circle games 67, 76
clap your hands, 67
clarinet 53
coda 46, 90, 95, 97, 132
coloratura soprano 53
Coltrane, John 154
compound meter 24, 25, 26, 64
concept (s) of music 7, 12, 14, 17, 60, 61, 79, 92, 98
concept formation 60
concrete operation (s) 61, 79
conjunct 29, 73
conservation 61
contour 29, 30, 34, 35, 48, 55, 57, 61, 64, 73, 74, 76 79, 80, 99, 136, 143
Copland, Aaron 48, 49, 56, 106, 139, 149, 156
creative movement 64
critical thinking 99
cultural literacy 144
Curwen hand signs 84, 90

D

Dalcroze 83, 98
Dance Macabre 100, 101, 133, 152

Davis, Miles 154
Debussy, Claude 127, 144, 149
descants 38, 39, 40, 42, 57
developmental aptitude 59
developmental stages 59, 60, 61, 69, 84, 87, 88
diatonic 85
digital synthesizer 52
disjunct 29, 30. 35
dotted patterns 22, 23, 24
duple meter 18, 64, 72
duration 19, 20, 21, 28, 57, 61, 79
dynamics 11, 12, 54, 55, 57, 60, 61, 79, 100, 101, 134, 137, 138, 149

E
echo clap (ping) 10, 12, 13
echo singing 9, 69
Eine Kleine Nachtmusik 47, 111, 150
elemental music 90
elements of music 7, 14, 17, 38, 54, 55, 57, 99, 104
Elliott, David 5, 8, 16
emotional effect 7
emotional reaction 14
exploring sound 50

F
finger plays 65, 70, 76
Firebird Suite, The 153
flute 51, 52
form 7, 10, 12, 13, 14, 17, 43, 44, 45, 46, 47, 48, 49, 57, 61, 78, 79
Four Seasons Suite, The 153
free movement 75, 76
free response 64
French horn 52, 148, 153

G
Gardner, Howard 6, 16, 59, 82
Gershwin, George 125, 149, 150
glissandos 97, 132
Gordon, Edwin 59, 60, 62, 63, 78, 82
greeting songs 112, 155
Greg and Steve 116, 119, 156
Grieg, Edvard 11,12, 13, 101, 150

H
harmony 7, 14, 17, 37, 38, 39, 40, 41, 42, 48, 54, 57, 59, 78, 98
Haydn 111
high and low 29, 34, 57, 61, 70, 99, 103
Hoe-Down 149, 156
homophonic 37, 38, 42

I
improvisation 91,92, 93, 94, 95
In the Hall of the Mountain King 11, 101, 150
inner hearing 86, 88, 89
integrating music 123
integration 124, 125, 130, 144
integrative categories 143
interval 29, 40, 63, 72

J
jazz 8, 23, 48, 77, 117, 140, 143, 144, 154

K
key signatures 34
Kind of Blue - The Miles Davis Quintet 154
Kodaly 71, 83, 84, 85, 86, 87, 88, 89, 90, 91, 100, 103, 104, 105, 106

L
language arts 59, 110, 123, 126, 130, 131, 133, 134, 155
Learning Basic Skills Through Music 119, 156
lesson plan 12, 98, 103, 104, 140
listening activity 11, 101, 102
listening guide 11, 106
listening lesson 99, 100, 105, 106, 130
listening map 100, 106
listening skill 100, 101
Liszt, Franz 133

M
major scale 32, 35, 12, 137
major triad 40, 41
McDonald and Simons 63, 70, 82
melodic patterns 9, 12, 14, 31, 33, 34, 35, 37, 64, 85, 86, 87, 89, 121, 125, 137

melodic perception 31

melody 7, 8, 9, 11, 12, 14, 17, 20, 24, 28, 29, 30, 31, 33, 34, 35, 37, 39, 41, 42, 48, 54, 55, 57, 61, 63, 71, 72, 74, 78, 79, 80, 97, 100, 101, 102, 105, 133, 136, 137, 150

meter 18, 21, 24, 25, 26, 28, 56, 57, 63, 64, 72, 80, 122, 136, 154

mezzo soprano 53

military music 139

minor scale 32, 33, 35, 36

minor triad 40, 41, 42, 57

modulation 55

movable do 31, 34, 35, 78, 84, 90, 100

movement 11, 14, 18, 28, 29, 30, 34, 35, 45, 46, 49, 55, 57, 60, 62, 63, 63, 64, 65, 66, 67, 68, 69, 75, 76, 79, 80, 89, 90, 91. 92, 93, 104, 117, 118, 119, 138

movement activities11, 13, 64, 81, 87, 99, 105, 111, 117, 118, 119

movement skill 63, 64, 65, 66, 78

Mozart 78, 111, 130, 139, 144, 150, 151, 154

Mozart Piano Concerto No. 21 in C 150

Mozart Symphony No. 40 in G minor 151

multimeter 25

Music and You 97, 103, 107

music and mathematics 124, 130, 157

music aptitude 60

music notation 33

music preference 7, 77

music reading 19, 90, 98, 104

music specialist 7, 9, 14, 117, 143, 144, 147, 155

music textbook series 97, 98, 99, 102, 104, 106, 107, 111, 142, 143, 144, 155

musical babble 62,

musical development 59, 60, 79, 80

musical intelligence 59

Mussorgsky, Modest 133, 138, 151, 155

mystery song 86, 87

O

Objectives 12, 97, 98, 103, 104

Objectives, expression 55

Objectives, form 48

Objectives, harmony 42

Objectives, melody 35

Objectives, rhythm 28

Objectives, timbre 53

oboe 52

Orff, Carl 83, 90, 91, 93, 94, 95, 96, 97, 98, 103, 104, 105, 106, 127, 128, 130, 126, 131, 133, 137, 138

ostinato 27, 38, 39, 42, 46, 57, 61, 76, 86, 87, 89, 90, 92, 93, 93, 95, 96, 97, 105, 137

P

Pachelbel's Canon 116, 151

Pachelbel, Johann 151

Palmer, Hap 12, 116, 119, 156

Parker, Charlie 154

partner songs 38, 39, 42, 57, 76

pentatonic 85, 112, 115, 116, 121, 132

pentatonic scale 33, 84, 85, 90, 93, 105, 121, 132, 137

percepts 7, 12, 14, 17, 21, 28, 29, 34, 57

perceptual development 28, 60, 69

perceptual skill (s) 7, 8, 17, 21, 28, 34, 41, 43, 50, 78, 80

percussion instruments 52, 53

performance directions 54, 55, 57

performance skill 7, 14, 42, 62, 95, 97

Peter and the Wolf 51, 54

Petrushka 25

phrase (s),10, 12, 13, 44, 45, 46, 48, 49, 55, 57, 62, 64, 70, 79, 86, 87, 89, 121, 137

Piaget 60, 61, 62, 82

Pictures at an Exhibition 54, 133, 138, 151

Piggy Back Songs 120

pitch matching 69, 75, 80

pitch syllables 31, 36

pizzicato 52

polymeter 25, 26, 27

polyphonic 37, 38, 42

popular music 8, 15, 17, 23, 25, 27, 43, 47, 52, 56, 72, 77, 78, 117, 140, 154

Prelude to the Afternoon of a Faun 127, 144, 149

preoperational 60, 61, 62, 77, 79

Prokofiev 51, 54
psychomotor 5, 6, 28, 117
pulse 9, 10, 12, 13, 18, 21, 22, 23, 24, 25,
    27, 28, 57, 62, 63, 67, 68, 75, 76, 79, 80,
    81, 116, 117, 120, 122
pulse accuracy 67

Q
question and answer phrases 44, 45, 46

R
Raffi 116, 156
reading melody 33
reform in education 6
Rhapsody in Blue 138, 150
rhythm 7, 8, 11, 12, 14, 17, 18, 19, 21, 25,
    27, 28, 37, 48, 54, 55, 57, 75, 96, 100,
    126, 127, 132, 137
rhythm patterns 8, 10, 13, 14, 19, 20, 21,
    22, 23, 25, 28, 31, 55, 59, 63, 68, 73, 75,
    85, 86, 87, 89, 91, 92, 93, 101, 104, 122,
    125
rhythm syllables 20, 24, 78, 85, 86, 90
rhythmic sensitivity 67
rhythmic skills 67, 89, 117
Rodeo 139, 149, 156
rondo 47, 48, 49, 57, 97, 136, 150, 154
round (s) 5, 10, 13, 14, 38, 39, 42, 57, 61,
    62, 76, 91

S
Saint-Saens, Camille 100, 133, 151
same and different 44, 45, 48, 49
saxophone 51, 155
scale (s) 31, 32, 31, 33, 34, 35, 36, 40, 57,
    112, 114, 121, 154
schema 57, 75
sensorimotor 56, 57, 58, 59, 65, 72, 74
set piece (s) 86, 91, 101
singing characteristics 59
singing games 59, 61, 62, 71, 76, 77, 106,
    112, 113
singing skill 64, 65, 66, 75, 100
singing voice 66, 67, 70
Smetana, Bedrich 127, 146
social studies 118, 119, 121, 124, 133,
    134, 135

soprano 49
stick notation 18, 20, 82, 83
Strauss, Richard 127, 145
Stravinsky, Igor 24, 121, 146
Suzuki 79
syncopation 20, 21, 22, 53, 68

T
tempo 5, 9, 10, 11, 51, 52, 56, 67, 70, 72,
    75, 82, 95, 97, 111, 131, 132, 141, 143,
    144
tenor 49
ternary 42, 43, 45, 46, 54
texture 35, 47, 49, 118, 120, 121, 123, 124
theme and variation 45, 46
Thus Spake Zarathustra 145
timbre 1, 5, 9, 10, 11, 15, 46, 47, 48, 49,
    50, 51, 52, 54, 56, 57, 60, 73, 75, 94, 97,
    128, 132
Time Out - The Dave Brubeck Quartet 148
tonal patterns 29, 33, 80, 81
tonality 29, 30, 32, 37, 39, 45, 54, 58, 59
tone poems 127, 146
tonic 30
triad (s) 37, 38, 39, 54
triple meter 16, 22, 24, 53, 68
trombone 49
trumpet 49
tuba 49
turning the phrase 42

U
unison 7, 10, 35, 39

V
Variations on a Shaker Theme 45, 143
verbal association 17, 29, 32, 53, 73, 75,
    84
viola 49
violin 46, 49
Vivaldi's Four Seasons 133, 137
Vivaldi, Antonio 133, 137, 146
vocal range 66, 67, 68, 70, 71, 72, 75, 76
volume 5, 51

W
waltz 16

Warren, Jean 114, 152
We All Live Together 114, 150
Weikart, Phyllis 63, 64, 76, 78
whole language 128, 129, 130, 151
woodwind instruments 48
word syllables 17, 18, 20, 29
World of Music, The 97, 107

X
xylophones 37, 38, 47, 86

Y
Young Person's Guide to the Orchestra, The 48, 54

SONG INDEX

A Ram Sam Sam 170
Acka Backa 10, 161
An Original Pentatonic Song 121
Autumn Leaves Are Falling 122
Bluebird 67, 162
Bow Wow Wow 166
Button 166
Can't Dance Josie 168
Charlie Over The Ocean 165
Chatter With The Angels 170
Clapping Land 169
Clap Your Hands 67
Ding Dong 170
Down Came A Lady 167
Going Outside 116
Grandma Grunts 167
Greetings 114
Hambone 93, 168
Hear Ye The Wind Is Rising 173
Hello 114
Hello Everybody 112
Hop Old Squirrel 163
Hot Cross Buns 39, 163
How Do You Do 113
Jim Along Josie 165
John Kanaka 119
Johnny Pounds with One Hammer 66
Kookaburra 10, 162

Kye Kye Kule 143
Lil Liza Jane 94, 164
Nobody's Home 173
Now the Day Is Done 115
Old Brass Wagon 171
Old Joe Clark 142
Old King Glory 163
Old Lady Sittin In The Dining Room 171
Oliver Twist 161
Original Pentatonic Song, An 121
Peas Porridge Hot 160
Punchinella 172
Rain Come Wet Me 96
Rocky Mountain 11, 166
Row Your Boat 165
Sally Go Round The Sun 164
Skin And Bones 174
Spring 122
Story Time 116
Teddy Bear 160
This Old Man 161
Together 113
Twenty Four Robbers 167
Wheels On The Bus, The 66
When Johnny Comes Marching Home 173
When The Train Comes Along 47, 172
Who's That 169
Zero 162